Dumpling Cats

Crochet & Collect Them All!

Sarah Sloyer

Dover Publications
Garden City, New York

For Iker

Bibliographical Note

Dumpling Cats: Crochet and Collect Them All! is a new work, first published by
Dover Publications in 2017.

International Standard Book Number
ISBN-13: 978-0-486-81343-1
ISBN-10: 0-486-81343-6

Printed in China by Chang Jiang Printing Media Co., Ltd.
81343608   2023
www.doverpublications.com

glossary

(U.S. terms)

BLO; back loops only: Work through only the back loops for as long as instructed.

Ch; chain: With a slipknot on your hook, yarn over and pull through.

Change color: When instructed to change colors, insert hook into stitch. Yarn over and pull through with your original color so there are two loops on your hook. Then, take your new color and pull it through both loops on your hook. Remember: This counts as one single crochet stitch! Continue with new color.
Note: When changing colors, cut previous color and tie your yarn tails in a knot.

Dec; single crochet decrease: Insert hook through the front loops of the next two stitches. Yarn over and pull through so there are two loops on your hook. Yarn over and pull through both loops to complete decrease.

Fasten off: After you finish your slip stitch, you'll need to fasten off the yarn and secure it so the stitch will not unravel. Cut the yarn leaving a few inches of tail. Then, with your hook, draw the tail through the loop on your hook. Remove hook and pull on tail to tighten. With a yarn needle, weave the tail through the stitches of the fabric to hide it.

FLO; front loops only: Work through only the front loops for as long as instructed.

HDC; half double crochet: Wrap working yarn over hook, insert into stitch, yarn over and pull through so there are three loops on your hook. Yarn over and pull through all three loops to complete stitch.

Inc; single crochet increase: Make two single crochet stitches in the same stitch.

Marker placement: Your stitch marker is always placed in the first stitch of every round. When starting an oval piece, work the foundation chain as instructed, then place the marker in the first stitch that you worked back into the foundation chain.

Parentheses; (   ): Repeat the stitches within the parentheses as many times as instructed.

Sc; single crochet: Insert hook into stitch, yarn over, pull through so you have two loops on your hook. Yarn over and pull through both loops to complete stitch.

Sl st; slip stitch: Insert hook into next stitch. Yarn over and pull through the loop on your hook. If fastening off, cut yarn and pull through.

contents

contents

Bonus Pattern!

tater

Rumor has it that Tater's actual name is something like Clyde or Dan; nobody can really remember for sure. He just bears such a striking resemblance to a tater tot that the nickname stuck. Thankfully, he's a friendly and easygoing fellow, so he doesn't mind.

FINISHED SIZE: 2¾in/7cm tall
(May vary depending on your hook size, yarn type, and tension)

SKILL LEVEL: Easy

MATERIALS

- Lion Brand® Vanna's Choice® 3.5oz/100g, 170yds/156m (100% acrylic)—one skein each: #806-100 White (Color A), #860-306 Tangerine Mist (Color B)
- Size D-3 (3.25mm) crochet hook
- Yarn needle
- 6mm safety eyes (2)
- Pink embroidery floss (for nose and mouth)
- Polyester stuffing
- Wooden stuffing stick
- Stitch markers and pins

Head and Body

In Color A:

Rnd 1: Ch 5. Starting in second ch from hook, sc 3. In 4th st, sc 4. On other side of foundation chain, sc 2. In 3rd st, sc 4—13 sts.

Rnd 2: Sc 4, sc 3 into next st, inc in next st, sc 5, inc in next st, sc 3 into next st—19 sts.

Rnd 3: In first st, change to Color B; sc 2 more in same st for a total of 3 sc in the first st. Sc 3 into next 3 sts, sc 2, inc in next 2 sts, sc 8, inc in next 2 sts, sc 1—31 sts.

Rnds 4–5: Sc in all 31 sts—31 sts.

Rnd 6: Sc 2, (inc in next st, sc 1) 5 times, sc in remaining 19 sts—36 sts. Pause here to place eyes and embroider nose and mouth. Eye placement: between Rnds 2–3, 6 sts apart.

Rnds 7–16: Sc in all 36 sts—36 sts.

Rnd 17: Sc 2, dec, (sc 4, dec) 5 times, sc 2—30 sts.

Rnd 18: (Sc 3, dec) 6 times—24 sts. Begin stuffing.

Rnd 19: Sc 1, dec, (sc 2, dec) 5 times, sc 1—18 sts.

Rnd 20: (Sc 1, dec) 6 times—12 sts. Continue stuffing.

Rnd 21: Dec in all sts—6 sts.

Fasten off with a slip stitch and use yarn needle to weave tail through the front loops of the remaining 6 stitches, pulling tightly to close the hole. Weave in tail.

Ears (Make 2)

In Color B:

Rnd 1: Start 6 sc in an adjustable ring—6 sts.

Rnd 2: (Sc 2, inc in next st) repeat 2 times—8 sts.

Rnd 3: Sc in all 8 sts—8 sts.

Rnd 4: (Sc 3, inc in next st) repeat 2 times—10 sts.

Rnd 5: Sc in all 10 sts—10 sts.

Fasten off with a slip stitch and leave a tail for sewing. Do not stuff.

Feet (Make 4)

In Color B:

Rnd 1: Start 5 sc in an adjustable ring—5 sts.

Rnd 2: Sc in all 5 sts—5 sts.

Fasten off with a slip stitch and leave a tail for sewing. Do not stuff.

Tail

In Color A:

Rnd 1: Start 6 sc in an adjustable ring—6 sts.

Rnds 2–3: Sc in all 6 sts—6 sts.

Rnd 4: In first st, change to Color B. Sc in remaining 5 sts—6 sts.

Rnds 5–7: Sc in all 6 sts—6sts.

Fasten off with a slip stitch and leave a tail for sewing. Do not stuff.

ASSEMBLY

Pin and sew pieces to body as shown.

waffles

Waffles spends most of her day lounging around in her cat bed with a good book. She's a voracious reader! She doesn't mind sharing her comfy spot, as long as you don't mind listening to her read out loud.

FINISHED SIZE: 2½in/6.5cm tall
(May vary depending on your hook size,
yarn type, and tension)

SKILL LEVEL: Intermediate

MATERIALS

- Lion Brand® Vanna's Choice® 3.5oz/100g,
  170yds/156m (100% acrylic)—one skein each:
  #860-100 White (Color A), #860-306 Tangerine
  Mist (Color B), #860-153 Black (Color C)
- Size D-3 (3.25mm) crochet hook
- Yarn needle
- 6mm safety eyes (2)
- Pink embroidery floss (for nose and mouth)
- Polyester stuffing
- Wooden stuffing stick
- Stitch markers and pins

Head

In Color A:

Rnd 1: Ch 4. Starting in 2nd ch from hook, sc
in next 2 sts. Sc 4 into next st. On other side of
foundation chain, sc 1. Sc 4 into next st—11 sts.

Rnd 2: Sc 10. In last st, change to Color B—11 sts.

Rnd 3: Sc 1. In next st, change to Color A. Sc in next
st, inc in next 3 sts, sc in next 2 sts, inc in next 2 sts.
Inc in last st, changing to Color B in second sc of
the increase—17 sts.

Rnd 4: Sc 3 into first st, sc 3 into second st,
changing to Color A in third sc. Sc 3 into next 2 sts.
Inc in next 3 sts. Sc in next 7 sts, inc in next st. Inc
in next st, changing to Color B in second sc of the
increase. Inc in last st—31 sts.

Rnd 5: Sc in first 5 sts. In next st, change to Color
C. Sc in next 7 sts. In next st, change to Color A. Sc
in next 15 sts. In next st, change to Color B. Sc in
next 2 sts—31 sts.

Rnd 6: Sc in first 2 sts. Inc in next st, sc 1. Inc in next
st, change to Color C in next st. (Inc in next st, sc
1) 3 times. Sc in next st. In next st, change to Color
A. Sc in next 14 sts. In next st, change to Color B.
Sc in next 2 sts—36 sts. Pause here to place eyes
and embroider nose and mouth. Eye placement:
between Rnds 3–4, approximately 4 sts apart.

Make a Cat Bed for your Dumpling Cat—
see Bonus Pattern on page 8

Rnd 7: Sc in first 7 sts, change to Color B in next st. Sc in next 10 sts, change to Color A in next st. Sc in next 14 sts. In next st, change to Color B. Sc in next 2 sts—36 sts.

Rnd 8: Sc in first 7 sts, change to Color B in next st. Sc in next 10 sts, change to Color A in next st. Sc in next 17 sts—36 sts.

Rnds 9–12: Continuing in Color A, sc in all 36 sts—36 sts.

Rnd 13: Sc 2, dec, (sc 4, dec) 5 times, sc 2—30 sts.

Rnd 14: (Sc 3, dec) 6 times—24 sts.

Rnd 15: Sc 1, dec, (sc 2, dec) 5 times, sc 1—18 sts. Begin stuffing.

Rnd 16: (Sc 1, dec) 6 times—12 sts.

Rnd 17: Dec in all sts—6 sts.

Fasten off with a slip stitch and use yarn needle to weave tail through the front loops of the remaining 6 stitches, pulling tightly to close the hole. Weave in tail.

Body

In Color C:

Rnd 1: Start 6 sc in an adjustable ring—6 sts.

Rnd 2: Inc in all 6 sts—12 sts.

Rnd 3: (Sc 1, inc in next st) 6 times—18 sts.

Rnd 4: Sc 1, inc in next st, (sc 2, inc in next st) 5 times, sc 1—24 sts.

Rnds 5–7: Change to Color B in first st. Sc in next 10 sts, change to Color A in next st. Sc in next 12 sts—24 sts.

Rnds 8–9: Change to Color C in first st. Sc in next 5 sts, change to Color B in next st, sc in next 4 sts, change to Color A in next st, sc in next 12 sts—24 sts.

Rnd 10: Change to Color B in first st. Sc in next 3 sts, dec. Sc in next 4 st, insert hook into **FLO** of next 2 st, YO with Color A and pull through to decrease, continuing with Color A. (Sc in next 4 sts, dec) 2 times—20 sts.

Fasten off with a slip stitch, leaving a tail for sewing. Stuff lightly.

Leg 1

In Color A:

Rnd 1: Start 6 sc in an adjustable ring—6 sts.

Rnds 2–3: Sc in all 6 sts—6 sts.

Rnd 4: Change to Color C in first st. Sc in remaining 5 sts—6 sts.

Rnds 5–6: Sc in all 6 sts—6 sts.

Fasten off with a slip stitch, leaving a tail for sewing. Do not stuff.

Leg 2 (Make 2)

In Color A:

Rnd 1: Start 6 sc in an adjustable ring—6 sts.

Rnds 2–6: Sc in all 6 sts—6 sts.

Fasten off with a slip stitch, leaving a tail for sewing. Do not stuff.

Leg 3

In Color C:

Rnd 1: Start 6 sc in an adjustable ring—6 sts.

Rnds 2–3: Sc in all 6 sts—6 sts.

Rnd 4: Change to Color A in first st. Sc in remaining 5 sts—6 sts.

Rnds 5–6: Sc in all 6 sts—6 sts.

Fasten off with a slip stitch, leaving a tail for sewing. Do not stuff.

Ears (Make 1 in Each Color)

In Colors B and C:

Rnd 1: Start 5 sc in an adjustable ring—5 sts.

Rnd 2: Sc 1, inc in next st, sc 2, inc in next st—7 sts.

Rnd 3: Sc in all 7 sts—7 sts.

Rnd 4: Sc 2, inc in next st, sc 3, inc in next st—9 sts.

Fasten off with a slip stitch and leave a tail for sewing. Do not stuff; press flat.

Tail

In Color C:

Rnd 1: Start 6 sc in an adjustable ring—6 sts.

Rnds 2–3: Sc in all 6 sts—6 sts.

Rnd 4: Change to Color B in first st. Sc in remaining 5 sts—6 sts.

Rnds 5–7: Sc in all 6 sts—6 sts.

Fasten off with a slip stitch, leaving a tail for sewing. Do not stuff.

ASSEMBLY

Pin and sew pieces to body as shown. Give the body additional stuffing as you sew it to the head.

cat 🐱 bed

Bonus Pattern!

FINISHED SIZE: 3½in/9cm by 1½in/4cm (May vary depending on your hook size, yarn type, and tension)

SKILL LEVEL: Easy

MATERIALS

- Lion Brand® Vanna's Choice® 3.5oz/100g, 170yds/156m (100% acrylic)—one skein: #860-173 Dusty Green (Color A), #860-123 Beige (Color B)
- Size D-3 (3.25mm) crochet hook
- Yarn needle
- Stitch markers and pins

Bed Edge

In Color A:

Rnd 1: Ch 45. Starting in second ch from hook, sc in next 43 sts. Sc 4 into next st. On other side of foundation ch, sc in next 42 sts. Sc 4 into next st—93 sts.

Rnds 2–7: Sc in all 93 sts—93 sts.

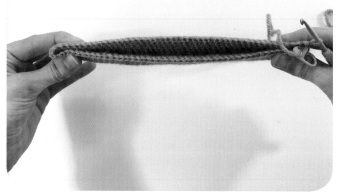

Yarn over and pull through to fasten off, leaving an extra long tail for sewing (about 20in/51cm long).

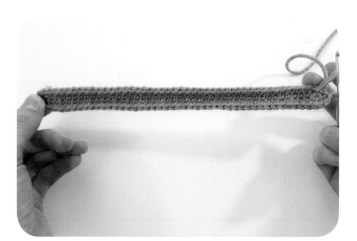

Note: Photo taken after Round 3.

Do not fasten off or stuff; press flat and close bottom by single crocheting through both sides.

Bed Bottom (Make 2)

In Color A:

Rnd 1: Ch 4. Starting in 2nd ch from hook, sc in next 2 sts. Sc 4 into next st. On other side of foundation chain, sc 1. Sc 4 into next st—11 sts.

Rnd 2: Sc 3, sc 3 into next st, inc in next st, sc 4, inc in next st, sc 3 into next st—17 sts.

Rnd 3: Sc 4, inc in next 3 sts, sc 6, inc in next 3 sts, sc 1—23 sts.

Rnd 4: Sc 5, (inc in next st, sc 1) 3 times, sc 6, (inc in next st, sc 1) 3 times—29 sts.

Rnd 5: Sc 6, (inc in next st, sc 2) 3 times, sc 5, (inc in next st, sc 2) 3 times—35 sts.

Rnd 6: Sc 7, (inc in next st, sc 3) 3 times, sc 5, (inc in next st, sc 3) 2 times, inc in next st, sc 2—41 sts.

Rnd 7: Sc 7, (inc in next st, sc 4) 3 times, sc 5, (inc in next st, sc 4) 2 times, inc in next st, sc 3–47 sts.

Rnd 8: Sc 8, (inc in next st, sc 5) 3 times, sc 4, (inc in next st, sc 5) 2 times, inc in next st, sc 4–53 sts.

After you finish the first bottom, fasten off and weave in tail. When you finish the second, do not fasten off. Remove the stitch marker and line up both bed bottoms, as shown, with the wrong sides facing in and the right sides facing out. Insert your hook through both layers and slip stitch in each stitch around to join the bottoms together. When the bottoms are joined, fasten off and weave in tail.

ASSEMBLY (BED BOTTOM)

Thread the leftover tail from the Bed Edge onto a yarn needle. Line the edge of the bed up along the bottom of the bed, as shown, leaving an opening of about 8 stitches.

Using the leftover yarn tail, whipstitch the two pieces together as shown. When the pieces are securely joined, weave in your yarn tail.

Bed Cushion

In Color B:

Rnd 1: Ch 4. Starting in 2nd ch from hook, sc in next 2 sts. Sc 4 into next st. On other side of foundation chain, sc 1. Sc 4 into next st—11 sts.

Rnd 2: Sc 3, sc 3 into next st, inc in next st, sc 4, inc in next st, sc 3 into next st—17 sts.

Rnd 3: Sc 4, inc in next 3 sts, sc 6, inc in next 3 sts, sc 1—23 sts.

Rnd 4: Sc 5, (inc in next st, sc 1) 3 times, sc 6, (inc in next st, sc 1) 3 times—29 sts.

Rnd 5: Sc 6, (inc in next st, sc 2) 3 times, sc 5, (inc in next st, sc 2) 3 times—35 sts.

Rnd 6: Sc 7, (inc in next st, sc 3) 3 times, sc 5, (inc in next st, sc 3) 2 times, inc in next st, sc 2—41 sts.

Rnd 7: Sc 7, (inc in next st, sc 4) 3 times, sc 5, (inc in next st, sc 4) 2 times, inc in next st, sc 3—47 sts.

Rnd 8: In **BLO** sc in all 47 sts—47 sts.

Rnd 9: Sc in all 47 sts—47 sts.

Rnd 10: In **BLO** sc 7, (dec, sc 4) 3 times, sc 5, (dec, sc 4) 2 times, dec, sc 3—41 sts.

Rnd 11: Sc 7, (dec, sc 3) 3 times, sc 5, (dec, sc 3) 2 times, dec in next st, sc 2—35 sts.

Rnd 12: Sc 6, (dec, sc 2) 3 times, sc 5, (dec, sc 2) 3 times—29 sts.

Rnd 13: Sc 5, (dec, sc 1) 3 times, sc 6, (dec, sc 1) 3 times—23 sts.

Rnd 14: (Sc 2, dec) 5 times, sc 3—18 sts.

Rnd 15: (Sc 1, dec) 6 times—12 sts.

Rnd 16: Dec in all sts—6 sts.

ASSEMBLY (BED CUSHION)

Do not stuff. Fasten off with a slip stitch and use yarn needle to weave tail through the front loops of the remaining 6 stitches, pulling tightly to close the hole. This is the bottom of the cushion. Weave in tail and press flat. Place in assembled bed, bottom facing down.

cheeks

The favorite time of day for Cheeks is lunchtime; he never wants it to end! So much so, in fact, that he likes to sneak extra food into his cheeks like a chipmunk and save it as a snack for later. Gross? Perhaps. Clever? Definitely.

FINISHED SIZE: 3in/7.5cm tall
(May vary depending on your hook size, yarn type, and tension)

SKILL LEVEL: Easy

MATERIALS

- Lion Brand® Vanna's Choice® 3.5oz/100g, 170yds/156m (100% acrylic)—one skein: #860-098 Fisherman (Color A)
- Size D-3 (3.25mm) crochet hook
- Yarn needle
- 6mm safety eyes (2)
- Pink embroidery floss (for nose and mouth)
- Polyester stuffing
- Wooden stuffing stick
- Stitch markers and pins

Head and Body

In Color A:

Rnd 1: Ch 10. Starting in second ch from hook, sc 8. In 9th st, sc 4. On other side of foundation chain, sc 7. In 8th st, sc 4—23 sts.

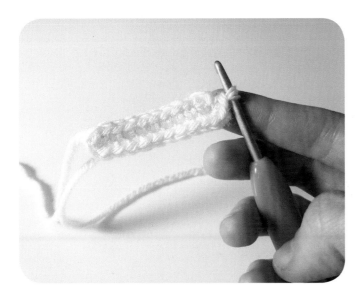

Rnd 2: Sc 9, (sc 3) in 10th st, inc in 11th st, sc 10, inc in next st, (sc 3) in next st—29 sts.

Rnds 3–4: Sc in all 29 sts—29 sts.

Rnd 5: (Sc 1, sc 3 into next st) 5 times, (sc 5, inc in next st) 3 times, sc 1—42 sts.

Rnd 6: Sc in all 42 sts—42 sts. Pause here to place eyes and embroider nose and mouth as in main photo. Eye placement: between Rnds 2–3, 4 sts apart.

Rnd 7: (Sc 6, inc in next st) 6 times—48 sts.

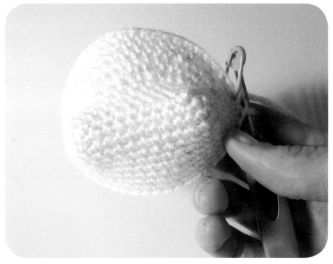

Rnds 8–20: Sc in all 48 st—48 sts.

Rnd 21: Sc 3, dec, (sc 6, dec) 5 times, sc 3—42 sts.

Rnd 22: (Sc 5, dec) 6 times—36 sts. Begin stuffing.

Rnd 23: Sc 2, dec, (sc 4, dec) 5 times, sc 2—30 sts.

Rnd 24: (Sc 3, dec) 6 times—24 sts.

Rnd 25: Sc 1, dec, (sc 2, dec) 5 times, sc 1—18 sts.

Rnd 26: (Sc 1, dec) 6 times—12 sts.

Rnd 27: Dec in all sts—6 sts.

Fasten off with a slip stitch and use yarn needle to weave tail through the front loops of the remaining 6 stitches, pulling tightly to close the hole. Weave in tail.

Ears (Make 2)

In Color A:

Rnd 1: Start 5 sc in an adjustable ring—5 sts.

Rnd 2: Sc 1, inc in next st, sc 2, inc in next st—7 sts.

Rnd 3: Sc in all 7 sts—7 sts.

Rnd 4: Sc 2, inc in next st, sc 3, inc in next st—9 sts.

Fasten off with a slip stitch and leave a tail for sewing. Do not stuff; press flat.

Tail

In Color A:

Rnd 1: Start 7 sc in an adjustable ring—7 sts.

Rnds 2–4: Sc in all 7 sts—7 sts.

Rnd 5: Sc 1, dec, sc 4—6 sts.

Rnds 6–8: Sc in all 6 sts—6 sts.

Fasten off with a slip stitch and leave a tail for sewing. Stuff lightly.

Feet (Make 4)

In Color A:

Rnd 1: Start 7 sc in an adjustable ring—7 sts.

Rnds 2–3: Sc in all 7 sts—7 sts.

Fasten off with a slip stitch and leave a tail for sewing. Do not stuff.

ASSEMBLY

Pin and sew pieces to body as shown.

food 🐱 bowls

FINISHED SIZE: 1½in/4cm diameter
(May vary depending on your hook size, yarn type, and tension)

SKILL LEVEL: Easy

MATERIALS

- Lion Brand® Vanna's Choice® 3.5oz/100g, 170yds/156m (100% acrylic)—one skein each: #860-183 Periwinkle (Color A), #860-104 Pink Grapefruit (Color B), #860-124 Toffee (Color C)
- Size D-3 (3.25mm) crochet hook
- Stitch markers and yarn needle

Empty Bowl

Bowl Top

In Color A:

Rnd 1: Start 6 sc in an adjustable ring—6 sts.

Rnd 2: Inc in all 6 sts—12 sts.

Rnd 3: (Sc 1, inc in next st) 6 times—18 sts.

Rnd 4: Sc 1, inc in next st, (sc 2, inc in next st) 5 times, sc 1—24 sts.

Rnds 5–6: Sc in all 24 sts—24 sts.

Fasten off with a slip stitch, leaving a tail long enough to weave in later.

Bowl Base

In Color A:

Rnd 1: Start 6 sc in an adjustable ring—6 sts.

Rnd 2: Inc in all 6 sts—12 sts.

Rnd 3: (Sc 1, inc in next st) 6 times—18 sts.

Rnd 4: Sc 1, inc in next st, (sc 2, inc in next st) 5 times, sc 1—24 sts.

Rnd 5: (Sc 5, inc in next st) 4 times—28 sts.

Rnd 6: In **BLO** sc in all 28 sts—28 sts.

Rnd 7: Sc 6, dec, sc 12, dec, sc 6—26 sts.

Rnd 8: (Sc 11, dec) 2 times—24 sts.

Do not fasten off. Place bowl top inside of bowl base. With your loop still on your hook, insert your hook into the next stitch and through the corresponding stitch in the bowl top. Complete a single crochet. Repeat in remaining 23 stitches. Fasten off and weave in ends.

Bowl with Food

Bowl Top

In Color B:

Rnd 1: Start 6 sc in an adjustable ring—6 sts.

Rnd 2: Inc in all 6 sts—12 sts.

Rnd 3: (Sc 1, inc in next st) repeat 6 times—18 sts.

Rnd 4: Sc 1, inc in next st, (sc 2, inc in next st) repeat 5 times, sc 1—24 sts.

Rnd 5: Sc in all 24 sts—24 sts.

Rnd 6: Sc in next 23 sts. In next st, change to Color C—24 sts.

Rnd 7: In **FLO** sc in all 24 sts—24 sts.

Drop loop from hook and put a marker in it to save your place. Do not fasten off or cut yarn. Turn bowl inside out, with wrong side facing out.

Bowl Base

In Color B:

Rnd 1: Start 6 sc in an adjustable ring—6 sts.

Rnd 2: Inc in all 6 sts—12 sts.

Rnd 3: (Sc 1, inc in next st) 6 times—18 sts.

Rnd 4: Sc 1, inc in next st, (sc 2, inc in next st) 5 times, sc 1—24 sts.

Rnd 5: (Sc 5, inc in next st) 4 times—28 sts.

Rnd 6: In **BLO** sc in all 28 sts—28 sts.

Rnd 7: Sc 6, dec, sc 12, dec, sc 6—26 sts.

Rnd 8: (Sc 11, dec) 2 times—24 sts.

Do not fasten off. Place bowl top inside of bowl base.

With your loop still on your hook, insert your hook into the next stitch and through the corresponding leftover front loop of Color B.

Complete a single crochet. Repeat in remaining 23 stitches. Fasten off and weave in ends.

Food

Pick up the loop of Color C you dropped after finishing Rnd 7 of the bowl top. Continue:

Rnd 1: (Sc 2, dec) repeat 6 times—18 sts.

Rnd 2: (Sc 1, dec) repeat 6 times—12 sts. Begin stuffing.

Rnd 3: Dec in all sts—6 sts.

Fasten off with a slip stitch and use yarn needle to weave tail through the front loops of the remaining 6 stitches, pulling tightly to close the hole. Weave in tail.

paula

Paula is like the Mama Bear of the cat household; she's always taking care of the other cats and is very protective of them. She also loves Broadway show tunes and sings them loudly throughout her day. You can hear her from down the block!

FINISHED SIZE: 3in/7.5cm tall
May vary depending on your hook size, yarn type, and tension)

SKILL LEVEL: Easy

MATERIALS

- Lion Brand® Vanna's Choice® 3.5oz/100g, 170yds/156m (100% acrylic)—one skein each: #860-100 White (Color A), #860-099 Linen (Color B)
- Size D-3 (3.25mm) crochet hook
- Yarn needle
- 6mm safety eyes (2)
- Pink embroidery floss (for nose and mouth)
- Black embroidery floss (for eyelashes)
- Polyester stuffing
- Wooden stuffing stick
- Stitch markers and pins

Head and Body

In Color A:

Rnd 1: Ch 5. Starting in second ch from hook, sc in next 3 sts. Sc 4 into next st. On other side of foundation chain, sc in next 2 sts. Sc 4 into next st—13 sts.

Rnd 2: Sc 4, sc 3 into next st, inc in next st, sc 5, inc in next st, sc 3 into next st—19 sts.

Rnd 3: In first st, change to B. Sc in remaining 18 sts—19 sts.

Rnd 4: Sc 5, inc in next 3 sts, sc 7, inc in next 3 sts, sc 1—25 sts.

Rnd 5: Sc 1, sc 3 into next 3 sts, sc 2, (inc in next st, sc 1) 3 times, sc 7, (inc in next st, sc 1) 3 times—37 sts.

Rnd 6: Sc 13, (inc in next st, sc 2) 3 times, sc 7, (inc in next st, sc 2) 2 times, inc in next st, sc 1—43 sts. Pause here to place eyes and embroider nose, mouth, and eyelashes. Eye placement: approximately 3–4 rounds up from center of foundation ch, 6 sts apart.

Rnds 7–20: Sc in all 43 sts—43 sts.

Rnd 21: Dec, sc in remaining 41 sts—42 sts.

Rnd 22: (Sc 5, dec) 6 times—36 sts.

Rnd 23: Sc 2, dec, (sc 1, dec) 5 times, sc 2—30 sts.

Rnd 24: (Sc 3, dec) 6 times—24 sts. Begin stuffing, continuing to stuff generously after each remaining round.

Rnd 25: Sc 1, dec, (sc 2, dec) 5 times, sc 1—18 sts.

Rnd 26: (Sc 1, dec) 6 times—12 sts.

Rnd 27: Dec in all sts—6 sts. Finish stuffing.

Fasten off with a slip stitch and use yarn needle to weave tail through the front loops of the remaining 6 stitches, pulling tightly to close the hole. Weave in tail.

Tail:

In Color A:

Rnd 1: Start 6 sc in an adjustable ring—6 sts.

Rnd 2: (Sc 1, inc in next st) 3 times—9 sts.

Rnd 3: Sc in all 9 sts—9 sts.

Rnd 4: In first st, change to Color B. Sc in remaining 8 sts—9 sts.

Rnd 5: Sc in all 9 sts—9 sts.

Rnd 6: Sc 1, dec, sc in remaining 6 sts—8 sts.

Rnd 7: Sc 3, dec, sc in remaining 3 sts—7 sts.

Rnd 8: Sc in all 7 sts—7 sts.

Fasten off with a slip stitch, leaving a tail for sewing. Stuff lightly.

Feet (Make 4)

In Color B:

Rnd 1: Start 5 sc in an adjustable ring—5 sts.

Rnds 2–3: Sc in all 5 sts—5 sts.

Fasten off with a slip stitch and leave a tail for sewing. Do not stuff.

Ears (Make 2)

In Color B:

Rnd 1: Start 5 sc in an adjustable ring—5 sts.

Rnd 2: Sc in all 5 sts—5 sts.

Rnd 3: Sc 1, inc in next st, sc 2, inc in next st—7 sts.

Rnd 4: Sc in all 7 sts—7 sts.

Fasten off with a slip stitch, leaving a tail for sewing. Do not stuff; press flat.

ASSEMBLY

Pin and sew pieces to body as shown.

dusty

Dusty's fur is actually white, but you'd never know it under all that dirt. He just can't stay clean! His sister, Blanche, gives him a bath every morning, but then he goes outside and always comes back a mess. Nobody knows what he gets into.

FINISHED SIZE: 3¼in/8.5cm tall
(May vary depending on your hook size, yarn type, and tension)

SKILL LEVEL: Easy

MATERIALS

- Lion Brand® Vanna's Choice® 3.5oz/100g, 170yds/156m (100% acrylic)—one skein: #860-400 Oatmeal (Color A)
- Size D-3 (3.25mm) crochet hook
- Yarn needle
- 6mm safety eyes (2)
- Pink embroidery floss (for nose and mouth)
- Polyester stuffing
- Wooden stuffing stick
- Stitch markers and pins

Head and Body

In Color A:

Rnd 1: Ch 5. Starting in second ch from hook, sc in next 3 sts. Sc 4 into next st. On other side of foundation chain, sc in next 2 sts. Sc 4 into next st—13 sts.

Rnd 2: Sc 4, sc 3 into next st, inc in next st, sc 5, inc in next st, sc 3 into next st—19 sts.

Rnd 3: Sc in all 19 sts—19 sts.

Rnd 4: Sc 5, inc in next 3 sts, sc 7, inc in next 3 sts, sc 1—25 sts.

Rnd 5: Sc in all 25 sts—25 sts.

Rnd 6: (Sc 4, inc in next st) 5 times—30 sts.

Rnd 7: Sc in all 30 sts—30 sts.

Rnd 8: Sc 2, inc in next st, (sc 4, inc in next st) 5 times, sc 2—36 sts.

Rnds 9–10: Sc in all 36 sts—36 sts.

Rnd 11: Sc 2, dec, (sc 4, dec) 5 times, sc 2—30 sts. Pause here to place eyes and embroider nose and mouth. Eye placement: approximately 8–9 rounds down from center of foundation ch, 5 sts apart.

Rnd 12: (Sc 3, dec) 6 times—24 sts.

Rnd 13: Sc 1, dec, (sc 2, dec) 5 times, sc 1—18 sts. Begin stuffing.

Rnd 14: (Sc 1, dec) 6 times—12 sts.

Rnd 15: Sc in all 12 sts—12 sts.

Rnd 16: (Sc 2, inc in next st) 4 times—16 sts.

Rnd 17: Sc in all 16 sts—16 sts.

Rnd 18: (Sc 3, inc in next st) 4 times—20 sts.

Rnd 19: Sc in all 20 sts—20 sts.

Rnd 20: (Sc 4, inc in next st) 4 times—24 sts.

Rnd 21: Sc in all 24 sts—24 sts.

Rnd 22: (Sc 2, dec) 6 times—18 sts.

Rnd 23: (Sc 1, dec) 6 times—12 sts.

Rnd 24: Dec in all sts—6 sts. Finish stuffing.

Fasten off with a slip stitch and use yarn needle to weave tail through the front loops of the remaining 6 stitches, pulling tightly to close the hole. Weave in tail.

Front Legs (Make 2)

In Color A:

Rnd 1: Start 5 sc in an adjustable ring—5 sts.

Rnds 2–4: Sc in all 5 sts—5 sts.

Do not stuff; press flat and close top with 2 single crochet stitches. Yarn over and pull through to fasten off, leaving a tail for sewing.

Back Legs (Make 2)

In Color A:

Rnd 1: Start 5 sc in an adjustable ring—5 sts.

Rnds 2–3: Sc in all 5 sts—5 sts.

Fasten off with a slip stitch and leave a tail for sewing. Do not stuff.

Ears (Make 2)

In Color A:

Rnd 1: Start 6 sc in an adjustable ring—6 sts.

Rnd 2: (Sc 2, inc in next st) 2 times—8 sts.

Rnd 3: Sc in all 8 sts—8 sts.

Rnd 4: (Sc 3, inc in next st) 2 times—10 sts.

Rnd 5: Sc in all 10 sts—10 sts.

Fasten off with a slip stitch and leave a tail for sewing. Do not stuff; press flat.

Tail

In Color A:

Rnd 1: Start 5 sc in an adjustable ring—5 sts.

Rnds 2–5: Sc in all 5 sts—5 sts.

Fasten off with a slip stitch and leave a tail for sewing. Do not stuff.

ASSEMBLY

Pin and sew pieces to body as shown.

blanche

Blanche is the resident clean freak of the household; her organizational skills are legendary. There's nothing she loves more than the smell of soap. Her biggest challenge of all is her perpetually filthy little brother, Dusty. She wishes he wouldn't go outside and get so messy, but she doesn't want to stifle his adventurer's spirit, so she lets him explore.

FINISHED SIZE: 4in/10cm tall
(May vary depending on your hook size, yarn type, and tension

SKILL LEVEL: Intermediate

MATERIALS

- Lion Brand® Vanna's Choice® 3.5oz/100g, 170yds/156m (100% acrylic)—one skein each: 860-100 White (Color A), 860-101 Pink (Color B)
- Size D-3 (3.25mm) crochet hook
- Yarn needle
- 6mm safety eyes (2)
- Pink embroidery floss (for nose and mouth)
- Black embroidery floss (for eyelashes)
- Polyester stuffing
- Wooden stuffing stick
- Stitch markers and pins

Head and Body

In Color A:

Rnd 1: Ch 6. Starting in second ch from hook, sc in next 4 sts. Sc 4 into next st. On other side of foundation chain, sc in next 3 sts. Sc 4 into next st—15 sts.

Rnd 2: Sc 5, sc 3 into next st, inc in next st, sc 6, inc in next st, sc 3 into next st—21 sts.

Rnd 3: Sc 6, inc in next 3 sts, sc 8, inc in next 3 sts, sc 1—27 sts.

Rnd 4: Sc in all 27 sts—27 sts.

Rnd 5: Sc 9, inc in next 3 sts, sc 10, inc in next 3 sts, sc 2—33 sts.

Rnd 6: Sc in all 33 sts—33 sts.

Rnd 7: Sc 10, inc in next 3 sts, sc 14, inc in next 3 st, sc 3—39 sts.

Rnds 8–9: Sc in all 39 sts—39 sts.

Rnd 10: Sc 11, dec 3 times, sc 13, dec 3 times, sc 3—33 sts.

Rnds 11–12: Sc in all 33 sts—33 sts. Pause here to place eyes and embroider nose, mouth, and eyelashes. Eye placement: between Rnds 9–10, 5 sts apart.

Rnd 13: Sc 10, dec 3 times, sc 10, dec 3 times, sc 1—27 sts.

Rnd 14: Sc 9, dec 2 times, sc 10, dec 2 times—23 sts.

Rnd 15: Sc 3, dec, (sc 2, dec) 4 times, sc 2—18 sts. Begin stuffing.

Rnd 16: (Sc 1, dec) repeat 6 times—12 sts.

Rnd 17: In **BLO** sc in all 12 sts—12 sts. The leftover loops will be used to join Color B and create Blanche's collar. But first, continue and complete the body:

Rnd 18: (Sc 2, inc in next st) repeat 4 times—16 sts.

Rnds 19–20: Sc in all 16 sts—16 sts.

Rnd 21: (Sc 7, inc in next st) 2 times—18 sts.

Rnd 22: Sc in all 18 sts—18 sts.

Rnd 23: (Sc 5, inc in next st) repeat 3 times—21 sts.

Rnd 24: Sc in all 21 sts—21 sts.

Rnd 25: Sc 3, inc in next st, (sc 6, inc in next st) 2 times, sc 3—24 sts.

Rnd 26: Sc in all 24 sts—24 sts.

Rnd 27: Sc 1, dec, (sc 2, dec) 5 times, sc 1—18 sts.

Rnd 28: (Sc 1, dec) 6 times—12 sts.

Rnd 29: Dec in all sts—6 sts. Finish stuffing.

Fasten off with a slip stitch and use yarn needle to weave tail through the front loops of the remaining 6 stitches, pulling tightly to close the hole. Weave in tail.

Collar

While holding the cat upside down, in first leftover front loop of Rnd 17, join Color B. Single crochet in all 12 stitches. Fasten off with a slip stitch and weave in ends.

Ears (Make 2)

In Color A:

Rnd 1: Start 5 sc in an adjustable ring—5 sts.

Rnd 2: Sc 1, inc in next st, sc 2, inc in next st—7 sts.

Rnd 3: Sc in all 7 sts—7 sts.

Rnd 4: Sc 2, inc in next st, sc 3, inc in next st—9 sts.

Fasten off with a slip stitch and leave a tail for sewing. Do not stuff; press flat.

Front Legs (Make 2)

In Color A:

Rnd 1: Start 5 sc in an adjustable ring—5 sts.

Rnds 2–6: Sc in all 5 sts—5 sts.

Do not stuff; press flat and close top with 2 single crochet stitches. Yarn over and pull through to fasten off, leaving a tail for sewing.

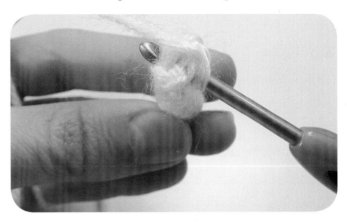

Back Legs (Make 2)

In Color A:

Rnd 1: Start 5 sc in an adjustable ring—5 sts.

Rnds 2–3: Sc in all 5 sts—5 sts.

Fasten off with a slip stitch and leave a tail for sewing. Do not stuff.

Tail

In Color A:

Rnd 1: Start 6 sc in an adjustable ring—6 sts.

Rnd 2: (Sc 1, inc in next st) 3 times—9 sts.

Rnd 3: Sc 1, inc in next st, (sc 2, inc in next st) 2 times, sc 1—12 sts.

Rnd 4: Sc in all 12 sts—12 sts.

Rnd 5: (Sc 2, inc in next st) 4 times—16 sts.

Rnd 6: Sc in all 16 sts—16 sts.

Rnd 7: (Sc 3, inc in next st) 4 times—20 sts.

Rnd 8: Sc in all 20 sts—20 sts.

Rnd 9: (Sc 3, dec) 4 times—16 sts.

Rnd 10: (Sc 2, dec) 4 times—12 sts. Begin stuffing.

Rnd 11: (Sc 1, dec) 4 times—8 sts.

Rnd 12: (Sc 2, dec) 2 times—6 sts.

Fasten off with a slip stitch and leave a tail for sewing.

ASSEMBLY

Pin and sew pieces to body as shown.

finneus

Finneus's favorite spot is the cardboard box near the kitchen; he likes to hide in there and wait until lunchtime so he can be first in line for food. If you don't get to your bowl fast enough, watch out—he might just nab your lunch before you get there!

FINISHED SIZE: 3½in/9cm tall
(May vary depending on your hook size, yarn type, and tension)

SKILL LEVEL: Easy

MATERIALS

- Lion Brand® Vanna's Choice® 3.5oz/100g, 170yds/156m (100% acrylic)—one skein: #860-149 Silver Gray (Color A)
- Size D-3 (3.25mm) crochet hook
- Yarn needle
- 6mm safety eyes (2)
- Pink embroidery floss (for nose and mouth)
- Polyester stuffing
- Wooden stuffing stick
- Stitch markers and pins

Head and Body

In Color A:

Rnd 1: Ch 5. Starting in second ch from hook, sc in next 3 sts. Sc 4 into next st. On other side of foundation chain, sc in next 2 sts. Sc 4 into next st—13 sts.

Rnd 2: Sc 4, sc 3 into next st, inc in next st, sc 5, inc in next st, sc 3 into next st—19 sts.

Rnd 3: Sc 5, inc in next 3 sts, sc 7, inc in next 3 sts, sc 1—25 sts.

Rnd 4: (Sc 4, inc in next st) 5 times—30 sts.

Rnds 5–6: Sc in all 30 st—30 sts

Rnd 7: Sc 2, inc in next st, (sc 4, inc in next st) 5 times, sc 2—36 sts.

Rnd 8: Sc in all 36 sts—36 sts.

Rnd 9: (Sc 5, inc in next st) 6 times—42 sts.

Rnds 10–11: Sc in all 42 sts—42 sts.

Rnd 12: (Sc 5, dec) 6 times—36 sts.

Rnd 13: Sc 2, dec, (sc 4, dec) 5 times, sc 2—30 sts.

Rnd 14: (Sc 3, dec) 6 times—24 sts. Pause here to place eyes and embroider nose and mouth. Eye placement between Rnds 8–9, 6 sts apart.

Rnd 15: (Sc 7, inc in next st) 3 times—27 sts.

Rnd 16: Sc 4, inc in next st, (sc 8, inc in next st) 2 times, sc 4—30 sts.

Rnd 17: (Sc 9, inc in next st) 3 times—33 sts.

Rnd 18: Sc in all 33 sts—33 sts.

Rnd 19: Sc 5, inc in next st, (sc 10, inc in next st) 2 times, sc 5—36 sts.

Rnds 20–23: Sc in all 36 sts—36 sts.

Rnd 24: Sc 2, dec, (sc 4, dec) 5 times, sc 2—30 sts.

Rnd 25: (Sc 3, dec) 6 times—24 sts.

Rnd 26: Sc 1, dec, (sc 2, dec) 5 times, sc 1—18 sts.

Rnd 27: (Sc 1, dec) 6 times—12 sts.

Rnd 28: Dec in all sts—6 sts.

Fasten off with a slip stitch and use yarn needle to weave tail through the front loops of the remaining 6 stitches, pulling tightly to close the hole. Weave in tail.

Back Legs (Make 2)

In Color A:

Rnd 1: Start 6 sc in an adjustable ring—6 sts.

Rnds 2–3: Sc in all 6 sts—6 sts.

Fasten off with a slip stitch, leaving a tail for sewing. Do not stuff.

Front Legs (Make 2)

In Color A:

Rnd 1: Start 6 sc in an adjustable ring—6 sts.

Rnds 2–4: Sc in all 6 sts—6 sts.

Do not stuff; press flat and close top with 2 single crochet stitches. Yarn over and pull through to fasten off, leaving a tail for sewing.

Ears (Make 2)

In Color A:

Rnd 1: Start 5 sc in an adjustable ring—5 sts.

Rnd 2: Sc in all 5 sts—5 sts.

Rnd 3: Sc 1, inc in next st, sc 2, inc in next st—7 sts.

Rnd 4: Sc in all 7 sts—7 sts.

Fasten off with a slip stitch, leaving a tail for sewing. Do not stuff; press flat.

Tail

In Color A:

Rnd 1: Start 6 sc in an adjustable ring—6 sts.

Rnds 2–7: Sc in all 6 sts—6 sts.

Fasten off with a slip stitch, leaving a tail for sewing. Stuff lightly.

ASSEMBLY

Pin and sew pieces to body as shown.

Make a Cardboard Box for your Dumpling Cat—
see Bonus Pattern on page 105

meatball

With his big body and his little legs, Meatball is clearly not a cat that was built for speed or mobility in general. That's fine, though, because he prefers to sit and stay in one place anyway, pondering life's big questions. He's quite the philosopher!

FINISHED SIZE: 2½in/6.5cm tall
(May vary depending on your hook size,
yarn type, and tension)

SKILL LEVEL: Easy

MATERIALS

- Lion Brand® Vanna's Choice® 3.5oz/100g,
  170yds/156m (100% acrylic)—one skein each:
  #860-100 White (Color A), #860-130 Honey
  (Color B)
- Size D-3 (3.25mm) crochet hook
- Yarn needle
- 6mm safety eyes (2)
- Dark brown embroidery floss
  (for nose and mouth)
- Cardboard (for base of cat)
- Polyester stuffing
- Wooden stuffing stick
- Stitch markers and pins

Body

In Color A:

Rnd 1: Ch 5. Starting in second ch from hook, sc
in next 3 sts. Sc 4 into next st. On other side of
foundation chain, sc in next 2 sts. Sc 4 into next
st—13 sts.

Rnd 2: Sc 4, sc 3 into next st, inc in next st, sc 5, inc
in next st, sc 3 into next st—19 sts.

Rnd 3: Sc 5, inc in next 3 sts, sc 7, inc in next 3 sts,
sc 1—25 sts.

Rnd 4: Sc 6, (inc in next st, sc 1) 3 times, sc 7, (inc in
next st, sc 1) 3 times—31 sts.

Rnd 5: (Sc 5, inc in next st) 5 times, sc 1—36 sts.

Rnd 6: (Sc 5, inc in next st) 6 times—42 sts.

Rnd 7: Sc 3, inc in next st, (sc 6, inc in next st)
5 times, sc 3—48 sts.

Rnd 8: (Sc 7, inc in next st) 6 times—54 sts.

Rnd 9: In **BLO** sc in all 54 sts—54 sts.

Rnds 10–12: Sc in all 54 sts—54 sts. Lightly trace
the base of your cat onto a piece of cardboard
and carefully cut it out. Place the cardboard
base into the base of the body, trimming to fit as
required.

Rnd 13: Sc 8, dec, (sc 16, dec) 2 times, sc 8—51 sts.

Rnd 14: (Sc 15, dec) 3 times—48 sts.

Rnd 15: Sc 7, dec, (sc 14, dec) 2 times, sc 7—45 sts.

Rnds 16–18: Sc in all 45 sts—45 sts.

Rnd 19: (Sc 13, dec) 3 times—42 sts.

Rnd 20: (Sc 5, dec) 6 times—36 sts.

Rnd 21: Sc 2, dec, (sc 4, dec) 5 times, sc 2—30 sts.

Rnd 22: (Sc 3, dec) 6 times—24 sts. Begin stuffing.

Rnd 23: Sc 1, dec, (sc 2, dec) 5 times, sc 1—18 sts.

Rnd 24: (Sc 1, dec) 6 times—12 sts.

Rnd 25: Dec in all sts—6 sts.

Fasten off with a slip stitch and use yarn needle to weave tail through the front loops of the remaining 6 stitches, pulling tightly to close the hole. Weave in tail.

Head

In Color B:

Rnd 1: Ch 5. Starting in second ch from hook, sc in next 3 sts. Sc 4 into next st. On other side of foundation chain, sc in next 2 sts. Sc 4 into next st—13 sts.

Rnd 2: Change to Color A in first st. Sc in next 3 sts, sc 3 into next st, inc in next st, sc 5, inc in next st, sc 3 into next st—19 sts.

Rnd 3: Sc 5, inc in next 3 sts, sc 7, inc in next 3 sts, sc 1—25 sts.

Rnd 4: (Sc 3 into next st, sc in next st) 3 times, sc in remaining 19 sts—31 sts.

Rnd 5: Sc 13, inc in next 2 sts, sc in next 12 sts, inc in next 2 sts, sc in next 2 sts—35 sts.

Rnds 6–8: Sc in all 35 sts—35 sts. Place eyes and embroider nose and mouth. Eye placement: between Rnds 2–3, approximately 8 sts apart.

Fasten off with a slip stitch and leave a tail for sewing. Stuff lightly.

Ears (Make 2)

In Color B:

Rnd 1: Start 5 sc in an adjustable ring—5 sts.

Rnd 2: Sc 1, inc in next st, sc 2, inc in next st—7 sts.

Rnd 3: Sc in all 7 sts—7 sts.

Rnd 4: Sc 2, inc in next st, sc 3, inc in next st—9 sts.

Rnd 5: Sc in all 9 sts—9 sts.

Fasten off with a slip stitch and leave a tail for sewing. Do not stuff; press flat.

Feet (Make 4)

In Color B:

Rnd 1: Start 6 sc in an adjustable ring—6 sts.

Rnds 2–3: Sc in all 6 sts—6 sts.

Fasten off with a slip stitch and leave a tail for sewing. Do not stuff.

Tail

In Color B:

Rnd 1: Start 6 sc in an adjustable ring—6 sts.

Rnds 2–4: Sc in all 6 sts—6 sts.

Rnd 5: Change to Color A in first st. Sc in remaining 5 sts—6 sts.

Rnds 6–7: Sc in all 6 sts—6 sts.

Fasten off with a slip stitch and leave a tail for sewing. Do not stuff.

ASSEMBLY

Pin and sew pieces to body as shown. Give the head additional stuffing as you sew it onto the body.

roly

Roly likes to spend most of his days outside in the grass, lying on his back and looking for pictures in the clouds. He only takes a break at dinnertime to eat, then goes back outside and stargazes late into the night.

FINISHED SIZE: 3½in/9cm tall
(May vary depending on your hook size, yarn type, and tension)

SKILL LEVEL: Easy

MATERIALS

- Lion Brand® Vanna's Choice® 3.5oz/100g, 170yds/156m (100% acrylic)—one skein each: #860-153 Black (Color A), #860-100 White (Color B)
- Size D-3 (3.25mm) crochet hook
- Yarn needle
- 6mm safety eyes (2)
- Pink embroidery floss (for nose and mouth)
- Polyester stuffing
- Wooden stuffing stick
- Stitch markers and pins

Body

In Color A:

Rnd 1: Ch 5. Starting in second ch from hook, sc in next 3 sts. Sc 4 into next st. On other side of foundation chain, sc in next 2 sts. Sc 4 into next st—13 sts.

Rnd 2: Sc 4, sc 3 into next st, inc in next st, sc 5, inc in next st, sc 3 into next st—19 sts.

Rnd 3: Sc 5, inc in next 3 sts, sc 7, inc in next 3 sts, sc 1—25 sts.

Rnds 4–5: Sc in all 25 sts—25 sts.

Rnd 6: Sc 10, dec, sc 11, dec—23 sts.

Rnd 7: Sc in all 23 sts—23 sts.

Rnd 8: Sc 9, dec, sc 7, dec, sc 3—21 sts.

Rnds 9–10: Sc in all 21 sts—21 sts.

Fasten off, leaving a tail for sewing. Stuff lightly.

Head

In Color B:

Rnd 1: Ch 5. Starting in second ch from hook, sc in next 3 sts. Sc 4 into next st. On other side of foundation chain, sc in next 2 sts. Sc 4 into next st—13 sts.

Rnd 2: Sc 1, sc 3 in next 2 sts, sc 1, inc in next st, sc 7, inc in next st—19 sts.

Rnd 3: Change to Color A in first st. Sc in remaining 18 sts—19 sts.

Rnd 4: Sc 2, sc 3 into next 4 sts, sc 3, inc in next 2 sts, sc 6, inc in next 2 sts—31 sts.

Rnd 5: Sc in all 31 sts—31 sts.

Rnd 6: (Sc 5, inc in next st) repeat 5 times, sc 1—36 sts. Pause here to place eyes and embroider nose and mouth. Eye placement: between Rnds 2–3, approximately 6 sts apart.

Rnds 7–10: Sc in all 36 sts—36 sts.

Rnd 11: Sc 2, dec, (sc 4, dec) 5 times, sc 2—30 sts.

Rnd 12: (Sc 3, dec) 6 times—24 sts.

Rnd 13: Sc 1, dec, (sc 2, dec) 5 times, sc 1—18 sts. Begin stuffing.

Rnd 14: (Sc 1, dec) 6 times—12 sts.

Rnd 15: Dec in all sts—6 sts.

Fasten off with a slip stitch and use yarn needle to weave tail through the front loops of the remaining 6 stitches, pulling tightly to close the hole. Weave in tail.

Feet (Make 4)

In Color B:

Rnd 1: Start 6 sc in an adjustable ring—6 sts.

Rnds 2–3: Sc in all 6 sts—6 sts.

Fasten off with a slip stitch and leave a tail for sewing. Do not stuff.

Ears (Make 2)

In Color A:

Rnd 1: Start 5 sc in an adjustable ring—5 sts.

Rnd 2: Sc 1, inc in next st, sc 2, inc in next st—7 sts.

Rnd 3: Sc in all 7 sts—7 sts.

Rnd 4: Sc 2, inc in next st, sc 3, inc in next st—9 sts.

Fasten off with a slip stitch and leave a tail for sewing. Do not stuff; press flat.

Tail

In Color B:

Rnd 1: Start 6 sc in an adjustable ring—6 sts.

Rnds 2–3: Sc in all 6 sts—6 sts.

Rnd 4: Change to Color A in first st. Sc in remaining 5 sts—6 sts.

Rnds 5–7: Sc in all 6 sts—6 sts.

Do not stuff; press flat and close top with 2 single crochet stitches. Yarn over and pull through to fasten off, leaving a tail for sewing.

ASSEMBLY

Pin and sew pieces to body as shown. Give the body additional stuffing as you sew it onto the head.

Continue with assembly.

chuck

Why is Chuck so grumpy? Nobody's sure—though some say it's because he is insecure over the fact that his younger brother, Boomer, is so much bigger than he is.

FINISHED SIZE: 4in/10cm tall
(May vary depending on your hook size, yarn type, and tension)

SKILL LEVEL: Easy

MATERIALS

- Lion Brand® Vanna's Choice® 3.5oz/100g, 170yds/156m (100% acrylic)—one skein: #860-125 Taupe
- Size D-3 (3.25mm) crochet hook
- Yarn needle
- 6mm safety eyes (2)
- Pink embroidery floss (for nose and mouth)
- Black embroidery floss (for eyebrows)
- Polyester stuffing
- Wooden stuffing stick
- Stitch markers and pins

Head and Body

In Color A:

Rnd 1: Ch 5. Starting in second ch from hook, sc in next 3 sts. Sc 4 into next st. On other side of foundation chain, sc in next 2 sts. Sc 4 into next st—13 sts.

Rnd 2: Sc 4, sc 3 into next st, inc in next st, sc 5, inc in next st, sc 3 into next st—19 sts.

Rnd 3: Sc 5, inc in next 3 sts, sc 7, inc in next 3 sts, sc 1—25 sts.

Rnd 4: Sc 6, (inc in next st, sc 1) 3 times, sc 7, (inc in next st, sc 1) 3 times—31 sts.

Rnd 5: Sc 7, (inc in next st, sc 2) 3 times, sc 6, (inc in next st, sc 2) 3 times—37 sts.

Rnds 6–9: Sc in all 37 sts—37 sts.

Rnd 10: Sc 16, inc in next 3 sts, sc 6, inc in next 3 sts, sc 9—43 sts.

Rnds 11–12: Sc in all 43 sts—43 sts.

Rnd 13: Sc 16, dec 3 times, sc 6, dec 3 times, sc 9—37 sts.

Rnd 14: Sc 2, dec, (sc 4, dec) 5 times, sc 3—31 sts.

Pause here to place eyes and embroider nose, mouth, and eyebrows. Eye placement: between Rnds 8–9, 5 sts apart.

Rnd 15: Sc 2, inc in next st, (sc 4, inc in next st) repeat 5 times, sc 3—37 sts. Begin stuffing the head.

Rnd 16: (Sc 5, inc in next st) 6 times, sc 1—43 sts.

Rnd 17: Sc in all 43 sts—43 sts.

Rnd 18: Sc 3, inc in next st, (sc 6, inc in next st) 5 times, sc 4—49 sts.

Rnds 19–22: Sc in all 49 sts—49 sts.

Rnd 23: (Sc 7, inc in next st) 6 times, sc 1—55 sts.

Rnds 24–25: Sc in all 55 sts—55 sts.

Rnd 26: (Sc 3, dec) 11 times—44 sts.

Rnd 27: Sc 1, dec, (sc 2, dec) 10 times, sc 1—33 sts.

Rnd 28: (Sc 1, dec) 11 times—22 sts. Begin stuffing the body.

Rnd 29: Sc 4, dec, (sc 3, dec) 3 times, sc 1—18 sts.

Rnd 30: (Sc 1, dec) 6 times—12 sts.

Rnd 31: Dec in all sts—6 sts.

Fasten off with a slip stitch and use yarn needle to weave tail through the front loops of the remaining 6 stitches, pulling tightly to close the hole. Weave in tail.

Ears (Make 2)

In Color A:

Rnd 1: Start 5 sc in an adjustable ring—5 sts.

Rnd 2: Sc 1, inc in next st, sc 2, inc in next st—7 sts.

Rnd 3: Sc in all 7 sts—7 sts.

Rnd 4: Sc 2, inc in next st, sc 3, inc in next sts—9 sts.

Rnd 5: Sc in all 9 sts—9 sts.

Fasten off with a slip stitch and leave a tail for sewing. Do not stuff; press flat.

Back Legs (Make 2)

In Color A:

Rnd 1: Start 8 sc in an adjustable ring—8 sts.

Rnds 2–4: Sc in all 8 sts—8 sts.

Fasten off, leaving a tail for sewing. Stuff lightly.

Front Legs (Make 2)

In Color A:

Rnd 1: Start 7 sc in an adjustable ring—7 sts.

Rnds 2–4: Sc in all 7 sts—7 sts.

Do not fasten off or stuff; press flat and close top with 3 single crochet stitches. Yarn over and pull through to fasten off, leaving a tail for sewing.

Tail

In Color A:

Rnd 1: Start 8 sc in an adjustable ring—8 sts.

Rnds 2–5: Sc in all 8 sts—8 sts.

Rnd 6: Sc 2, dec, sc in remaining 4 sts—7 sts.

Rnd 7: Sc in all 7 sts—7 sts.

Fasten off, leaving a tail for sewing. Stuff lightly.

ASSEMBLY:

Pin and sew pieces to body as shown.

boomer

Don't let Boomer's size intimidate you. Although he's the largest cat of the bunch, he's also one of the friendliest. He spends most of his day in front of the TV, and recently figured out how to use the DVR, which he uses to record all of the other cats' favorite programs. Just don't try to change the channel while he is watching his competitive dance shows (they're his favorite).

FINISHED SIZE: 4in/10cm tall
(May vary depending on your hook size, yarn type, and tension)

SKILL LEVEL: Intermediate

MATERIALS

- Lion Brand® Vanna's Choice® 3.5oz/100g, 170yds/156m (100% acrylic)—one skein each: #860-130 Honey (Color A), #860-126 Chocolate (Color B)
- Size D-3 (3.25mm) crochet hook
- Yarn needle
- 6mm safety eyes (2)
- Dark brown embroidery floss (for nose and mouth)
- Polyester stuffing
- Wooden stuffing stick
- Stitch markers and pins

Head and Body

Starting in Color A:

Rnd 1: Ch 5. Starting in second ch from hook, sc in next 3 sts. Sc 4 into next st. On other side of foundation chain, sc in next 2 sts. Sc 4 into next st—13 sts.

Rnd 2: Sc 4, sc 3 into next st, inc in next st, sc 5, inc in next st, sc 3 into next st—19 sts.

Rnd 3: Sc 5, inc in next 3 st, sc 7, inc in next 3 st, sc 1—25 sts.

Rnd 4: Sc 6, (inc in next st, sc 1) 3 times, sc 7, (inc in next st, sc 1) 3 times—31 sts.

Rnd 5: Sc 7, (inc in next st, sc 2) 3 times, sc 6, (inc in next st, sc 2) 3 times—37 sts.

Rnds 6–7: Sc in all 37 sts—37 sts.

Rnd 8: Sc 8, (inc in next st, sc 3) 3 times, sc 6, (inc in next st, sc 3) 2 times, inc in next st, sc 2—43 sts.

Rnd 9: Sc 40, change to Color B in next st, sc 2—43 sts.

Rnd 10: Sc 9, change to Color A in next st, sc 8, inc in next 4 sts, sc 7, inc in next 4 sts, sc 8, change to Color B in next st, sc 2—51 sts.

Rnd 11: Sc 9, change to Color A in next st, sc in remaining 41 sts—51 sts.

Rnd 12: Sc in all 51 sts—51 sts.

Rnd 13: Sc 18, dec 4 times, sc 7, dec 4 times, sc 10—43 sts. Pause here to place eyes and embroider nose and mouth. Eye placement: 9–10 rounds down from top of head, approximately 3–4 sts apart.

Rnd 14: Sc 3, inc, (sc 6, inc) 5 times, sc 1, change to Color B in next st, sc 2—49 sts.

Rnd 15: Sc 13, change to Color A in next st, sc in next 32 sts, change to Color B in next st, sc 2—49 sts.

Rnd 16: Sc 7, inc in next st, sc 5, change to Color A in next st, sc 1, inc in next st, (sc 7, inc in next st) 4 times, sc 1—55 sts.

Rnds 17–18: Sc in all 55 sts—55 sts.

Rnd 19: Sc 4, inc in next st, (sc 8, inc in next st) 5 times, sc 1, change to Color B in next st, sc 3—61 sts.

Rnd 20: Sc 19, change to Color A in next st, sc in next 37 sts, change to Color B in next st, sc 3—61 sts.

Rnd 21: Sc 19, change to Color A in next st, sc in remaining 41 sts—61 sts.

Rnd 22: (Sc 9, inc in next st) 6 times, sc 1—67 sts.

Rnds 23–28: Sc in all 67 sts—67 sts.

Rnd 29: Sc 2, dec, (sc 4, dec) 10 times, sc 3—56 sts.

Rnd 30: (Sc 3, dec) 11 times, sc 1—45 sts.

Rnd 31: Sc 1, dec, (sc 2, dec) 10 times, sc 2—34 sts. Begin stuffing.

Rnd 32: (Sc 1, dec) 11 times, sc 1—23 sts.

Rnd 33: (Sc 2, dec) 5 times, sc 3—18 sts.

Rnd 34: (Sc 1, dec) 6 times—12 sts.

Rnd 35: Dec in all sts—6 sts.

Fasten off with a slip stitch and use yarn needle to weave tail through the front loops of the remaining 6 stitches, pulling tightly to close the hole. Weave in tail.

Back Legs (Make 2)

In Color A:

Rnd 1: Start 8 sc in an adjustable ring—8 sts.

Rnds 2–4: Sc in all 8 sts—8 sts.

Fasten off with a slip stitch and leave a tail for sewing. Stuff lightly.

Front Legs (Make 2)

In Color A:

Rnd 1: Start 7 sc in an adjustable ring—7 sts.

Rnds 2–4: Sc in all 7 sts—7 sts.

Do not fasten off or stuff; press flat and close top with 3 single crochet stitches. Yarn over and pull through to fasten off, leaving a tail for sewing.

Ears (Make 2)

In Color A:

Rnd 1: Start 5 sc in an adjustable ring—7 sts.

Rnd 2: Sc 1, inc in next st, sc 2, inc in next st—7 sts.

Rnd 3: Sc in all 7 sts—7 sts.

Rnd 4: Sc 2, inc in next st, sc 3, inc in next st—9 sts.

Fasten off with a slip stitch and leave a tail for sewing. Do not stuff; press flat.

Tail

In Color B:

Rnd 1: Start 8 sc in an adjustable ring—8 sts.

Rnd 2: Sc in all 8 sts—8 sts.

Rnd 3: Change to Color A in first st. Sc in remaining 7 sts—8 sts.

Rnds 4–5: Sc in all 8 sts—8 sts.

Rnd 6: Change to Color B in first st. Sc 2, dec, sc in remaining 3 sts—7 sts.

Rnd 7: Sc in all 7 sts—7 sts.

Rnd 8: Change to Color A in first st. Sc in remaining 6 sts—7 sts.

Rnds 9–10: Sc in all 7 sts.

Fasten off with a slip stitch and leave a tail for sewing. Stuff lightly.

ASSEMBLY

Pin and sew pieces to body as shown.

wilbur

Wilbur dreams of flying; he read somewhere on the Internet that bumblebees shouldn't be able to fly, but they manage to defy physics. Is this true? Don't know, but Wilbur finds it inspirational, and he has decided that the bumblebee is his new spirit animal. If a bumblebee can fly, perhaps a cat can too!

FINISHED SIZE: 3in/7.5cm tall
(May vary depending on your hook size, yarn type, and tension)

SKILL LEVEL: Intermediate

MATERIALS

- Lion Brand® Vanna's Choice® 3.5oz/100g, 170yds/156m (100% acrylic)—one skein each: #860-149 Silver Gray (Color A), #860-153 Black (Color B), #860-158 Mustard (Color C), #860-105 Silver Blue (Color D)
- Size D-3 (3.25mm) crochet hook
- Yarn needle
- 6mm safety eyes (2)
- Pink embroidery floss (for nose and mouth)
- Polyester stuffing
- Wooden stuffing stick
- Stitch markers and pins

Rnd 8: In **FLO** sc in all 34 sts—34 sts.

Rnd 9: In remaining back loops of Rnd 8: (Sc 16, inc in next st) 2 times—36 sts.

Head and Body

In Color A:

Rnd 1: Ch 4. Starting in 2nd ch from hook, sc in next 2 sts. Sc 4 into next st. On other side of foundation chain, sc 1. Sc 4 into next st—11 sts.

Rnd 2: Sc in all 11 sts—11 sts.

Rnd 3: Sc 3, inc in next 3 sts, sc 2, inc in next 3 sts—17 sts.

Rnd 4: Sc 3 into first 4 sts, sc in next st, inc in next 2 sts, sc 8, inc in next 2 sts—29 sts.

Rnd 5: Sc in all 29 sts—29 sts.

Rnd 6: Sc 2, (inc in next st, sc 1) 5 times, sc 17—34 sts.

Rnd 7: Change to Color B in first st. Sc in remaining 33 sts—34 sts. Pause here to place eyes and embroider nose and mouth. Eye placement: between Rnds 3–4, approximately 6 sts apart.

Rnd 10: (Sc 5, inc in next st) 4 times. Sc 4, change to Color C in next st, inc in next sc, sc in next 5 sts, inc in last st—42 sts.

Rnds 11–12: Sc in all 42 sts—42 sts.

Rnd 13: Sc 33, change to Color B in next st, sc in next 8 sts—42 sts.

Rnds 14–15: Sc in all 42 sts—42 sts.

Rnd 16: Sc 33, change to Color C in next st, sc in next 8 sts—42 sts.

Rnd 17: Sc in all 42 sts—42 sts.

Rnd 18: Sc 33, change to Color B in next st, sc in next 8 sts—42 sts.

Rnd 19: Sc in all 42 sts—42 sts.

Rnd 20: (Sc 5, dec) 6 times—36 sts.

Rnd 21: Sc 2, dec, (sc 4, dec) 4 times, sc in next st, change to Color C in next st, sc 2, dec, sc 2—30 sts.

Rnd 22: (Sc 3, dec) 6 times—24 sts. Begin stuffing, continuing to stuff generously in the following rounds.

Rnd 23: Sc 1, dec, (sc 2, dec) 5 times, sc 1—18 sts.

Rnd 24: (Sc 1, dec) repeat 6 times—12 sts.

Rnd 25: Dec in all sts—6 sts.

Fasten off with a slip stitch and use yarn needle to weave tail through the front loops of the remaining 6 stitches, pulling tightly to close the hole. Weave in tail.

Ears (Make 2)

In Color A:

Rnd 1: Start 5 sc in an adjustable ring—5 sts.

Rnd 2: Sc 1, inc in next st, sc 2, inc in next st—7 sts.

Rnd 3: Sc in all 7 sts—7 sts.

Rnd 4: Sc 2, inc in next st, sc 3, inc in next st—9 sts.

Rnd 5: Sc in all 9 sts—9 sts.

Fasten off with a slip stitch and leave a tail for sewing. Do not stuff; press flat.

Feet (Make 4)

In Color A:

Rnd 1: Start 6 sc in an adjustable ring—6 sts.

Rnds 2–3: Sc in all 6 sts.

Fasten off with a slip stitch and leave a tail for sewing. Do not stuff.

Tail

In Color A:

Rnd 1: Start 7 sc in an adjustable ring—7 sts.

Rnds 2–5: Sc in all 7 sts—7 sts.

Rnd 6: Sc 2, dec, sc in next 3 sts—6 sts.

Rnd 7: Sc in all 6 sts—6 sts.

Fasten off with a slip stitch and leave a tail for sewing. Stuff lightly.

Wings (Make 2)

In Color D:

Rnd 1: Start 6 sc in an adjustable ring—6 sts.

Rnd 2: Inc in all 6 sts—12 sts.

Rnd 3: Sc in all 12 sts—12 sts.

Rnd 4: (Sc 4, dec) 2 times—10 sts.

Rnd 5: (Sc 3, dec) 2 times—8 sts.

Do not fasten off or stuff; press flat and close top with 3 single crochet stitches. Yarn over and pull through to fasten off, leaving a tail for sewing.

ASSEMBLY

Pin and sew pieces to body as shown.

daisy

Daisy is very gentle and quiet. She has such a tiny voice, you can barely hear her most of the time. That's why she prefers to spend most of her time outside in the garden, conversing with the flowers; they speak very quietly, too.

FINISHED SIZE: 3in/7.5cm tall
(May vary depending on your hook size, yarn type, and tension)

SKILL LEVEL: Intermediate

MATERIALS

- Lion Brand® Vanna's Choice® 3.5oz/100g, 170yds/156m (100% acrylic)—one skein each: #860-123 Beige (Color A), #860-171 Fern (Color B), #860-130 Honey (Color C), #860-101 Pink (Color D)
- Size D-3 (3.25mm) crochet hook
- Yarn needle
- 6mm safety eyes (2)
- Pink embroidery floss (for nose and mouth)
- Polyester stuffing
- Wooden stuffing stick
- Stitch markers and pins

Rnd 10: In remaining back loops of Rnd 9: Change to Color A in first st. Sc in next 15 sts, inc in next st. Sc in next 16 sts, inc in next st—36 sts.

Rnd 11: (Sc 5, inc in next st) 5 times—42 sts. Pause here to place eyes and embroider nose and mouth. Eye placement: between Rnds 3–4, approximately 6 sts apart.

Head and Body

In Color A:

Rnd 1: Ch 4. Starting in 2nd ch from hook, sc in next 2 sts. Sc 4 into next st. On other side of foundation chain, sc 1. Sc 4 into next st—11 sts.

Rnd 2: Sc in all 11 sts—11 sts.

Rnd 3: Sc 3, inc in next 3 sts, sc 2, inc in next 3 sts—17 sts.

Rnd 4: Sc 3 into first 4 sts, sc in next st, inc in next 2 sts, sc 8, inc in next 2 sts—29 sts.

Rnd 5: Sc in all 29 sts—29 sts.

Rnd 6: Sc 2, (inc in next st, sc 1) 5 times, sc 17—34 sts.

Rnd 7: Sc in next 33 sts. In last st, change to Color B—34 sts.

Rnd 8: Sc in all 34 sts—34 sts.

Rnd 9: In **FLO** sc in all 34 sts—34 sts.

Rnd 12: Sc in all 42 sts—42 sts.

Rnds 13–14: Sc 1, change to Color C in next st, sc in next 20 sts, change to Color A in next st, sc in next 19 sts—42 sts.

Rnds 15–16: Sc in all 42 sts—42 sts.

Rnds 17–18: Sc 1, change to Color C in next st, sc in next 20 sts, change to Color A in next st, sc in next 19 sts—42 sts.

Rnd 19: Sc in all 42 sts—42 sts.

Rnd 20: (Sc 5, dec) 6 times—36 sts.

Rnd 21: Sc 2, dec, (sc 4, dec) 5 times, sc 2—30 sts.

Rnd 22: (Sc 3, dec) 6 times—24 sts. Begin stuffing, continuing to stuff generously in the following rounds.

Rnd 23: Sc 1, dec, (sc 2, dec) 5 times, sc 1—18 sts.

Rnd 24: (Sc 1, dec) 6 times—12 sts.

Rnd 25: Dec in all sts—6 sts.

Fasten off with a slip stitch and use yarn needle to weave tail through the front loops of the remaining 6 stitches, pulling tightly to close the hole. Weave in tail.

Flower Petals (Make 9)

In Color D:

Rnd 1: Start 6 sc in an adjustable ring—6 sts.

Rnd 2: Inc in all 6 sts—12 sts.

Rnd 3: Sc in all 12 sts—12 sts.

Rnd 4: (Sc 4, dec) 2 times—10 sts.

Rnd 5: (Sc 3, dec) 2 times—8 sts.

Do not fasten off or stuff; press flat and close top with 3 single crochet stitches. Yarn over and pull through to fasten off, leaving a tail for sewing.

Ears (Make 2)

In Color A:

Rnd 1: Start 5 sc in an adjustable ring—5 sts.

Rnd 2: Sc 1, inc in next st, sc 2, inc in next st—7 sts.

Rnd 3: Sc in all 7 sts—7 sts.

Rnd 4: Sc 2, inc in next st, sc 3, inc in next st—9 sts.

Do not fasten off or stuff; press flat and close top with 4 single crochet stitches. Yarn over and pull through to fasten off, leaving a tail for sewing.

Feet (Make 4)

In Color A:

Rnd 1: Start 6 sc in an adjustable ring—6 sts.

Rnds 2–3: Sc in all 6 sts—6 sts.

Fasten off with a slip stitch and leave a tail for sewing. Do not stuff.

Tail

In Color B:

Rnd 1: Start 7 sc in an adjustable ring—7 sts.

Rnd 2: Sc in all 7 sts—7 sts.

Rnd 3: Change to Color A in first st. Sc in remaining 6 sts—7 sts.

Rnd 4: Sc in all 7 sts—7 sts.

Rnd 5: Change to Color B in first st. Sc in remaining 6 sts—7 sts.

Rnd 6: Sc 2, dec, sc in next 3 sts—6 sts.

Rnd 7: Change to Color A in first st. Sc in remaining 5 sts—6 sts.

Rnd 8: Sc in all 6 sts—6 sts.

Fasten off with a slip stitch and leave a tail for sewing. Stuff lightly.

ASSEMBLY

Pin and sew pieces to body as shown. Sew flower petals to head between Rnds 10–11.

Sew ears to head between Rnds 7–8.

Feet placement:

misty

True to her name, Misty is, well, mysterious. No one knows where she came from, and her tail doesn't seem to be just a costume. She doesn't say much, either. But she makes a really good omelet, so the other cats are fine with her staying.

FINISHED SIZE: 4in/10cm tall
(May vary depending on your hook size, yarn type, and tension)

SKILL LEVEL: Intermediate

MATERIALS

- Lion Brand® Vanna's Choice® Baby 3.5oz/100g, 170yds/156m (100% acrylic)—one skein: #840-168 Mint (Color A)
- Lion Brand® Vanna's Choice® 3.5oz/100g, 170yds/156m (100% acrylic)—one skein: #860-098 Fisherman (Color B)
- Size D-3 (3.25mm) crochet hook
- Yarn needle
- 6mm safety eyes (2)
- Pink embroidery floss (for nose and mouth)
- Black embroidery floss (for eyelashes)
- Polyester stuffing
- Wooden stuffing stick
- Stitch markers and pins

Tail

In Color A:

Rnd 1: Start 6 sc in an adjustable ring—6 sts.

Rnd 2: Sc in all 6 sts—6 sts.

Rnd 3: Sc 1, inc in next st, sc 1, slst 3—7 sts.

Rnd 4: Sc in all 7 sts—7 sts.

Rnd 5: Sc 2, inc in next st, sc 2, slst 2—8 sts.

Rnd 6: Slst 2, sc 5, inc in next st—9 sts.

Rnd 7: Sc 1, inc in next st, sc 2, inc in next st, sc 1, slst 3—11 sts.

Rnd 8: Slst 3, sc 6, inc in next st, sc 1—12 sts.

Rnd 9: Inc in first st, sc 1, inc in next st, sc 3, inc in next st, sc 2, slst 3—15 sts.

Rnd 10: Slst 6, sc 6, inc in next st, sc 2—16 sts.

Rnd 11: Inc in first st, sc 2, inc in next st, sc 5, inc in next st, sc 3, slst 3—19 sts.

Rnd 12: Slst 8, sc 9, inc in next st, sc 1—20 sts.

Rnd 13: Sc 1, inc in next st, sc 2, inc in next st, sc 7, inc in next st, sc 4, slst 3—23 sts.

Rnd 14: Slst 10, sc 10, inc in next st, sc 2—24 sts.

Rnd 15: Sc 1, inc in next st, sc 3, inc in next st, sc 3, inc in next st, sc 5, inc in next st, sc 5, slst 3—28 sts.

Rnd 16: Slst 16, sc in remaining 12 sts—28 sts.

Rnd 17: (Inc in first st, sc 3) 2 times, inc in next st, sc in remaining 19 sts—31 sts.

Rnd 18: Sc 22. Fasten off in next stitch (9 sts away from marker)—31 sts.

Body and Head
(continued from tail)

With Color B, make a slipknot on your hook. Insert hook into the back loop of the stitch where you fastened off and join yarn. Place marker here. This will now be the beginning of your new rounds. Continue:

Rnd 19: In **BLO** sc in all 31 sts—31 sts.

Rnd 20: Sc 8, slst 19, sc 4—31 sts.

Rnd 21: Sc 12, inc in next st, sc 3, inc in next st, sc 3, inc in next st, sc 7, dec, sc 1—33 sts.

Rnd 22: Dec, sc 1, dec, sc 6, slst 16, sc 6—31 sts.

Rnd 23: Sc 14, inc in next st, sc 3, inc in next st, sc 6, dec, sc 2, dec—31 sts.

Rnd 24: (Sc 2, dec) 2 times, sc 4, slst 14, dec, sc 1, dec—27 sts. Begin stuffing.

Rnd 25: (Sc 1, dec) 2 times, sc 5, (inc in next st, sc 2) 2 times, inc in next st, sc 5, dec 2 times—26 sts.

Rnd 26: Dec 3 times, sc 2, slst 12, sc 2, dec 2 times—21 sts.

Rnd 27: Dec 2 times, (inc in next st, sc 1) 8 times, inc in last st—28 sts.

Rnd 28: (Sc, inc in next st) 2 times, (sc 3, inc in next st) 6 times—36 sts.

Rnd 29: (Sc 5, inc in next st) 6 times—42 sts.

Rnds 30–31: Sc in all 42 sts—42 sts.

Rnd 32: Sc 33, dec, sc 3, dec, sc 2—40 sts.

Rnd 33: Sc 1, dec, sc 3, dec, sc 6, dec, sc 5, dec, sc 6, dec, sc 4, slst 5—35 sts.

Rnd 34: Slst 8, sc 22, dec, sc 1, dec—33 sts.

Rnd 35: (Sc 1, dec) 3 times, sc 21, inc in next st, sc 1, inc in next st—32 sts.

Rnd 36: (Sc 1, inc) 3 times, sc in remaining 26 sts—35 sts.

Rnd 37: (Sc 5, dec) 5 times—30 sts. Pause here to place eyes and embroider nose, mouth, and eyelashes. Eye placement: between Rnds 27–28, approximately 6 sts apart.

Rnd 38: Sc 2, dec, (sc 4, dec) 4 times, sc 2—25 sts.

Rnd 39: (Sc 3, dec) 5 times—20 sts.

Rnd 40: Sc 1, dec, (sc 2, dec) 4 times, sc 1—15 sts.

Rnd 41: (Sc 1, dec) 5 times—10 sts.

Rnd 42: Dec in all sts—5 sts.

Fasten off with a slip stitch and use yarn needle to weave tail through the front loops of the remaining 6 stitches, pulling tightly to close the hole. Weave in tail.

Ridge

With Color A, make a slipknot on your hook. Insert your hook into the first leftover front loop of Rnd 20 and join yarn. Single crochet in all 31 stitches. Fasten off and weave in ends.

Tail Fins (Make 2)

In Color A:

Rnd 1: Start 5 sc in an adjustable ring—5 sts.

Rnd 2: Sc 1, inc in next st, sc 2, inc in next st—7 sts.

Rnd 3: Sc in all 7 sts—7 sts.

Rnd 4: Sc 1, dec, sc 2, dec—5 sts.

Do not fasten off or stuff; press flat and close top with 2 single crochet stitches. Yarn over and pull through to fasten off, leaving a tail for sewing.

Ears (Make 2)

In Color B:

Rnd 1: Start 5 sc in an adjustable ring—5 sts.

Rnd 2: Sc 1, inc in next st, sc 2, inc in next st—7 sts.

Rnd 3: Sc in all 7 sts—7 sts.

Rnd 4: Sc 2, inc in next st, sc 3, inc in next st—9 sts.

Rnd 5: Sc in all 9 sts—9 sts.

Fasten off with a slip stitch and leave a tail for sewing. Do not stuff; press flat.

Legs (Make 2)

In Color B:

Rnd 1: Start 6 sc in an adjustable ring—6 sts.

Rnds 2–8: Sc in all 6 sts—6 sts.

Do not fasten off or stuff; press flat and close top with 2 single crochet stitches. Yarn over and pull through to fasten off, leaving a tail for sewing.

ASSEMBLY

Pin and sew pieces to body as shown.

minerva

Minerva dressed up as a witch last Halloween and loved the costume so much, she never took it off. Since then, she likes to spend her time in the kitchen concocting strange potions. She swears her powers are real; she managed to turn Todd into a frog three months ago and he hasn't changed back!

FINISHED SIZE: 5½in/14cm tall
(May vary depending on your hook size, yarn type, and tension)

SKILL LEVEL: Intermediate

MATERIALS

- Lion Brand® Vanna's Choice® 3.5oz/100g, 170yds/156m (100% acrylic)—one skein each: #860-153 Black (Color A), #860-145 Eggplant (Color B), #860-151 Charcoal Gray (Color C)
- Size D-3 (3.25mm) crochet hook
- Yarn needle
- 6mm safety eyes (2)
- Pink embroidery floss (for nose and mouth)
- Polyester stuffing
- Wooden stuffing stick
- Stitch markers and pins

Hat and Head

In Color A:

Rnd 1: Start 6 sc in an adjustable ring—6 sts.

Rnd 2: (Sc 2, inc in next st) 2 times—8 sts.

Rnd 3: Sc in all 8 sts—8 sts.

Rnd 4: (Sc 3, inc in next st) 2 times—10 sts.

Rnd 5: Sc in all 10 sts—10 sts.

Rnd 6: Change to Color B in first st, sc 1, inc in next st, (sc 2, inc in next st) 2 times, sc 1—13 sts.

Rnd 7: Sc in all 13 sts—13 sts.

Rnd 8: (Sc 2, inc in next st) 4 times, sc 1—17 sts.

Rnd 9: Sc in all 17 sts—17 sts.

Rnd 10: Change to Color A in first st, sc 2, inc in next st, (sc 3, inc in next st) 3 times, sc 1—21 sts.

Rnd 11: Sc in all 21 sts—21 sts.

Rnd 12: (Sc 3, inc in next st) 5 times, sc 1—26 sts.

Rnd 13: Sc in all 26 sts—26 sts.

Rnd 14: Change to Color B in first st, (sc 5, inc in next st) 4 times, sc 1—30 sts.

Rnd 15: Sc in all 30 sts—30 sts.

Rnd 16: Sc 7, inc in next st, (sc 6, inc in next st) 3 times, sc 1—34 sts.

Rnd 17: In **FLO** change to Color A in first st, sc in next 5 sts, inc in next st, (sc 4, inc in next st) 5 times, sc 2—40 sts.

Drop loop from hook and place an extra marker in it to save your spot. This will be the beginning of the brim of the hat, which you can return to after finishing the head. To continue the head, make a slipknot of Color C on your hook. In the first leftover back loop of Rnd 17, insert your hook, join yarn and continue.

Rnd 18: (Sc 16, inc in next st) 2 times—36 sts. Move your original stitch marker to the first stitch of this round.

Rnds 19–23: Sc in all 36 sts—36 sts.

Pause here to place eyes and embroider nose and mouth as shown on next page. Eye placement: 4–5 rnds down from bottom of hat, 5 sts apart.

Rnd 24: Sc 2, dec, (sc 4, dec) 5 times, sc 2—30 sts. Begin stuffing.

Rnd 25: (Sc 1, dec) 10 times—20 sts.

Rnd 26: (Sc 2, dec) 5 times—15 sts.

Rnd 27: (Sc 1, dec) 5 times—10 sts. Pause here and drop loop from hook, placing an extra marker in it to save your spot. You will now create the brim of the hat before continuing onto the body.

Hat Brim
(continued from Rnd 17 of hat and head):

Pick up the dropped loop of Color A.

Rnd 1: (Sc 7, inc in next st) 5 times—45 sts.

Rnd 2: Sc 4, inc in next st, (sc 8, inc in next st) 4 times, sc 4—50 sts.

Rnd 3: (Sc 9, inc in next st) 5 times—55 sts.

Rnd 4: Sc 5, inc in next st, (sc 10, inc in next st) 4 times, sc 5—60 sts.

Rnd 5: (Sc 11, inc in next st) 5 times—65 sts.

Rnd 6: Sc 6, inc in next st, (sc 12, inc in next st) 4 times, sc 6—70 sts.

Fasten off with a slip stitch and weave in tail.

Body and Dress
(continued from Rnd 27 of hat and head):

Pick up dropped loop and continue:

Rnd 28: In **FLO** change to Color A in first st, sc in remaining 9 sts—10 sts.

Rnd 29: (Sc 1, inc in next st) 5 times—15 sts.

Rnd 30: Sc in all 15 sts—15 sts.

Rnd 31: (Sc 4, inc in next st) 3 times—18 sts.

Rnd 32: Sc in all 18 sts—18 sts.

Rnd 33: (Sc 5, inc in next st) 3 times—21 sts.

Rnd 34: Sc in all 21 sts—21 sts.

Rnd 35: (Sc 6, inc in next st) 3 times—24 sts.

Drop loop from hook and place an extra marker in it to save your place. You will continue the dress later, but first you will finish the body underneath. Make a slipknot of Color C on your hook, join yarn and continue.

Rnd 36: In **BLO** sc in each st—24 sts. Place a marker in the first st of round.

Rnd 37: (Sc 2, dec) 6 times—18 sts.

Rnd 38: (Sc 1, dec) 6 times—12 sts. Begin stuffing.

Rnd 39: Dec in all sts—6 sts.

Fasten off with a slip stitch and use yarn needle to weave tail through the front loops of the remaining 6 stitches, pulling tightly to close the hole. Weave in tail.

Pick up the loop you dropped at the end of Rnd 35 and continue the dress:

Rnd 40: In remaining front loops left over from Rnd 36, sc in all 24 sts—24 sts.

Rnd 41: (Sc 5, inc in next st) 4 times—28 sts.

Rnd 42: Sc in all 28 sts—28 sts.

Fasten off with a slip stitch and weave in tail.

Front Legs (Make 2)

In Color C:

Rnd 1: Start 6 sc in an adjustable ring—6 sts.

Rnds 2–3: Sc in all 6 sts—6 sts.

Rnd 4: Change to Color A in first st. Sc in remaining 5 sts—6 sts.

Rnds 5–7: Sc in all 6 sts—6 sts.

Do not fasten off or stuff; press flat and close top with 2 single crochet stitches. Yarn over and pull through to fasten off, leaving a tail for sewing.

Back Legs (Make 2)

In Color C:

Rnd 1: Start 6 sc in an adjustable ring—6 sts.

Rnds 2–3: Sc in each st—6 sts.

Do not fasten off or stuff; press flat and close top with 2–3 single crochet stitches. Yarn over and pull through to fasten off, leaving a tail for sewing.

Tail

In Color C:

Rnd 1: Start 6 sc in an adjustable ring—6 sts.

Rnds 2–7: Sc in all 6 sts—6 sts.

Fasten off with a slip stitch, leaving a tail for sewing. Stuff lightly.

Ears (Make 2)

In Color C:

Rnd 1: Start 5 sc in an an adjustable ring—5 sts.

Rnd 2: Sc 1, inc in next st, sc 2, inc in next st—7 sts.

Rnd 3: Sc in all 7 sts—7 sts.

Do not stuff; press flat and close top with 3 single crochet stitches. Yarn over and pull through to fasten off, leaving a tail for sewing.

ASSEMBLY

Pin and sew legs to body as shown. Stitch front legs onto body approximately 3 rounds down from the head. Sew ears to hat as shown.

todd

Minerva claims she turned Todd into a frog three months ago using one of her spells. Truth is, Todd put on a frog costume and simply couldn't reach the zipper to take it off again. He plays along, though, because he doesn't want to hurt her feelings.

FINISHED SIZE: 3½in/9cm tall
(May vary depending on your hook size,
yarn type, and tension)

SKILL LEVEL: Intermediate

MATERIALS

- Lion Brand® Vanna's Choice® 3.5oz/100g,
170yds/156m (100% acrylic)—one skein each:
#860-305 Pearl Mist (Color A), #860-171 Fern
(Color B), #860-153 Black (Color C), #860-100
White (Color D)

- Size D-3 (3.25mm) crochet hook

- Yarn needle

- 6mm safety eyes (2)

- Pink embroidery floss (for nose and mouth)

- Polyester stuffing

- Wooden stuffing stick

- Stitch markers and pins

Head

In Color A:

Rnd 1: Ch 4. Starting in 2nd ch from hook, sc
in next 2 sts. Sc 4 into next st. On other side of
foundation chain, sc 1. Sc 4 into next st—11 sts.

Rnd 2: Sc 3, sc 3 into next st, inc in next st, sc 4, inc
in next st, sc 3 into next st—17 sts.

Rnd 3: Sc 4, inc in next 3 sts, sc 6, inc in next 3 sts,
sc 1—23 sts.

Rnd 4: Inc in first 4 sts, sc 3, inc in next st, sc 11, inc
in next st, sc 3—29 sts. Pause here to place eyes
and embroider nose and mouth as in main photo.
Eye placement: between Rnds 1–2, approximately
3 sts apart.

Rnd 5: Sc 28, in last st, change to Color B—29 sts.

Rnd 6: (Sc 6, inc in next st) 4 times, sc 1—33 sts.

Rnd 7: In **FLO** sc in all 33 sts—33 sts.

Rnd 8: In leftover back loops from Rnd 7: Sc 1,
inc in next st, (sc 2, inc in next st) 2 times, sc in 25
remaining sts—36 sts.

Rnds 9–14: Sc in all 36 sts—36 sts.

Rnd 15: Sc 2, dec, (sc 4, dec) 5 times, sc 2—30 sts.

Rnd 16: (Sc 3, dec) 6 times—24 sts.

Rnd 17: Sc 1, dec, (sc 2, dec) 5 times, sc 1—18 sts. Begin stuffing.

Rnd 18: (Sc 1, dec) 6 times—12 sts.

Rnd 19: Dec in all sts—6 sts.

Fasten off with a slip stitch and use yarn needle to weave tail through the front loops of the remaining 6 stitches, pulling tightly to close the hole. Weave in tail.

Frog Eyes

In Color C:

Rnd 1: Start 4 sc in an adjustable ring—4 sts.

Rnd 2: Insert hook into first of the 4 sts. Change to Color D in first st. In same spot, sc 1 (two sc in first st). Place marker in the first of the 2 sts. Inc in remaining 3 sts—8 sts.

Rnd 3: Sc 1, change to Color B in next st, sc 1, inc in next st, sc 3, inc in next st—10 sts.

Rnd 4: Dec in all sts—5 sts.

Do not stuff. Fasten off with a slip stitch and use yarn needle to weave tail through the front loops of the remaining 5 stitches, pulling tightly to close the hole. Weave in tail through the center of the hole and out through the bottom of the eye.

Body

In Color A:

Rnd 1: Ch 5. Starting in second ch from hook, sc in next 3 sts. Sc 4 into next st. On other side of foundation chain, sc in next 2 sts. Sc 4 into next st—13 sts.

Rnd 2: Sc 4, sc 3 into next st, inc in next st, sc 5, inc in next st, sc 3 into next st—19 sts.

Rnds 3–4: Sc in all 19 sts—19 sts.

Rnd 5: Change to Color B in first st, sc in remaining 18 sts—19 sts.

Rnd 6: In **FLO** sc in all 19 sts—19 sts.

Rnd 7: In remaining back loops of Rnd 6, sc in all 19 sts—19 sts.

Rnd 8: Sc 7, dec, sc 8, dec—17 sts.

Rnd 9: Sc in all 17 sts—17 sts.

Fasten off with a slip stitch and leave a tail for sewing. Stuff lightly.

Back Legs (Make 2)

In Color A:

Rnd 1: Start 5 sc in an adjustable ring—5 sts.

Rnds 2–3: Sc in all 5 sts—5 sts.

Fasten off with a slip stitch and leave a tail for sewing. Do not stuff.

Front Legs (Make 2)

In Color A:

Rnd 1: Start 5 sc in an adjustable ring—5 sts.

Rnds 2–4: Sc in all 5 sts—5 sts.

Rnd 5: Change to Color B in first st, sc in remaining 4 sts—5 sts.

Rnd 6: Sc in all 5 sts—5 sts.

Do not stuff; press flat and close top with 2 single crochet stitches. Yarn over and pull through to fasten off, leaving a tail for sewing.

Tail

In Color A:

Rnd 1: Start 5 sc in an adjustable ring—5 sts.

Rnds 2–5: Sc in all 5 sts—5 sts.

Fasten off with a slip stitch and leave a tail for sewing. Do not stuff.

ASSEMBLY

Pin and sew pieces to body as shown.

reggie

Roar! What Reggie lacks in size he makes up for in his voice. He is not quite as loud as Paula yet, but he's training tirelessly in hopes of surpassing her. One day, he'll be the loudest cat in the house!

FINISHED SIZE: 3½in/9cm tall
(May vary depending on your hook size,
yarn type, and tension)

SKILL LEVEL: Intermediate

MATERIALS

- Lion Brand® Vanna's Choice® 3.5oz/100g,
  170yds/156m (100% acrylic)—one skein each:
  #860-123 Beige (Color A), #860-158 Mustard
  (Color B), #860-130 Honey (Color C)
- Size D-3 (3.25mm) crochet hook
- Yarn needle
- 6mm safety eyes (2)
- Pink embroidery floss (for nose and mouth)
- Polyester stuffing
- Wooden stuffing stick
- Stitch markers and pins

Head

Starting in Color A:

Rnd 1: Ch 4. Starting in 2nd ch from hook, sc
in next 2 sts. Sc 4 into next st. On other side of
foundation chain, sc 1. Sc 4 into next st—11 sts.

Rnd 2: Sc 3, sc 3 into next st, inc in next st, sc 4, inc
in next st, sc 3 into next st—17 sts.

Rnd 3: Sc 4, inc in next 3 sts, sc 6, inc in next 3 sts,
sc 1—23 sts.

Rnd 4: Inc in first 4 sts, sc 3, inc in next st, sc 11, inc
in next st, sc 3—29 sts.

Rnd 5: Sc 28, in last st, change to Color B—29 sts.

Rnd 6: (Sc 6, inc in next st) 4 times, sc 1—33 sts.

Rnd 7: In **FLO** sc in all 33 sts—33 sts.

Rnd 8: In leftover back loops from Rnd 7: In first st,
change to Color C. Do not cut Color B. Sc in all 33
sts—33 sts.

Rnd 9: In **FLO** sc in all 33 sts—33 sts.

When you complete Rnd 9, drop your loop from
your hook and place an extra stitch marker in it to
save your spot. Make a slipknot of Color B on your
hook. In the first leftover back loop of Rnd 9, join
yarn and continue.

Rnd 10: In leftover back loops of Rnd 9: (Sc 10, inc
in next st) 3 times—36 sts. Place stitch marker in
first st of this round. Refer to photo on next page.
Pause here to place eyes and embroider nose and
mouth as in main photo. Eye placement: between
Rnds 1–2, 3 sts apart.

Rnd 2: In leftover back loops of Rnd 1, (Sc 1 in next st, ch 6, reinsert hook into same st, slst) in each st around.

Rnds 11–14: Sc in all 36 sts—36 sts.

Rnd 15: Sc 2, dec, (sc 4, dec) 5 times, sc 2—30 sts.

Rnd 16: (Sc 3, dec) 6 times—24 sts.

Rnd 17: Sc 1, dec, (sc 2, dec) 5 times, sc 1—18 sts. Begin stuffing.

Rnd 18: (Sc 1, dec) 6 times—12 sts.

Rnd 19: Dec in all sts—6 sts.

Fasten off with a slip stitch and use yarn needle to weave tail through the front loops of the remaining 6 stitches, pulling tightly to close the hole. Weave in tail.

Mane

Pick up the loop of Color C that you dropped at the end of Rnd 9.

Rnd 1: In **FLO** (sc 1 in next st, ch 6, re-insert hook into same st, slst) in each st around.

Fasten off with a slip stitch and weave in yarn.

Ears (Make 2)

In Color B:

Rnd 1: Start 6 sc in an adjustable ring—6 sts.

Rnds 2–3: Sc in each st—6 sts.

Do not stuff; press flat and close top with 3 single crochet stitches. Yarn over and pull through to fasten off, leaving a tail for sewing.

Body

In Color A:

Rnd 1: Ch 5. Starting in second ch from hook, sc in next 3 sts. Sc 4 into next st. On other side of foundation chain, sc in next 2 sts. Sc 4 into next st—13 sts.

Rnd 2: Sc 4, sc 3 into next st, inc in next st, sc 5, inc in next st, sc 3 into next st—19 sts.

Rnds 3–4: Sc in all 19 sts—19 sts.

Rnd 5: Change to Color B in first st, sc in remaining 18 sts—19 sts.

Rnd 6: In **FLO** sc in all 19 sts—19 sts.

Rnd 7: In remaining back loops of Rnd 6, sc in all 19 sts—19 sts.

Rnd 8: Sc 7, dec, sc 8, dec—17 sts.

Fasten off with a slip stitch, leaving a tail for sewing. Stuff lightly.

Front Legs (Make 2)

In Color A:

Rnd 1: Start 5 sc in an adjustable ring—5 sts.

Rnds 2–3: Sc in all sts—5 sts.

Rnd 4: Change to Color B in first st, sc in remaining 4 sts—5 sts.

Rnds 5–7: Sc in all 5 sts—5 sts.

Do not fasten off or stuff; press flat and close top with 2 single crochet stitches. Yarn over and pull through to fasten off, leaving a tail for sewing.

Back Legs (Make 2)

In Color A:

Rnd 1: Start 5 sc in an adjustable ring—5 sts.

Rnds 2–3: Sc in all 5 sts—5 sts.

Fasten off with a slip stitch and leave a tail for sewing. Do not stuff.

Tail

In Color A:

Rnd 1: Start 5 sc in an adjustable ring—5 sts.

Rnds 2–5: Sc in all 5 sts—5 sts.

Fasten off with a slip stitch and leave a tail for sewing. Do not stuff.

ASSEMBLY

Pin and sew body to head as shown.

Sew ears to head at Rnd 7.

Sew other parts to body as shown.

ruby

Why is Ruby dressed as a ladybug? No reason in particular, really—she just wanted a snazzy-looking outfit to dance in, and she liked the color of this costume the most.

FINISHED SIZE: 3in/7.5cm tall
(May vary depending on your hook size, yarn type, and tension)

SKILL LEVEL: Intermediate

MATERIALS

- Lion Brand® Vanna's Choice® 3.5oz/100g, 170yds/156m (100% acrylic)—one skein each: #860-100 White (Color A), #860-153 Black (Color B), #860-113 Scarlet (Color C)
- Size D-3 (3.25mm) crochet hook
- Yarn needle
- 6mm safety eyes (2)
- Pink embroidery floss (for nose and mouth)
- Black embroidery floss (for eyelashes)
- Polyester stuffing
- Wooden stuffing stick
- Stitch markers and pins

Head and Body

In Color A:

Rnd 1: Ch 4. Starting in 2nd ch from hook, sc in next 2 sts. Sc 4 into next st. On other side of foundation chain, sc 1. Sc 4 into next st—11 sts.

Rnd 2: Sc in all 11 sts—11 sts.

Rnd 3: Sc 3, inc in next 3 sts, sc 2, inc in next 3 sts—17 sts.

Rnd 4: Sc 3 into first 4 sts, sc in next st, inc in next 2 sts, sc 8, inc in next 2 sts—29 sts.

Rnd 5: Sc in all 29 sts—29 sts.

Rnd 6: Sc 2, (inc in next st, sc 1) 5 times, sc 17—34 sts.

Rnd 7: Change to Color B in first st. Sc in remaining 33 sts—34 sts. Pause here to place eyes and embroider nose, mouth, and eyelashes. Eye placement: between Rnds 3–4, approximately 6 sts apart.

Rnd 8: In **FLO** sc in all 34 sts—34 sts.

Rnd 9: In remaining back loops of Rnd 8, sc in first 4 sts. To make first antenna: Sc in next 6 sts, in next st make second antenna as per first. Sc in next 4 sts, inc in next st, sc in next 16 sts, inc in next st—36 sts.

Rnd 10: In first st, change to Color C. Sc in remaining 35 sts—36 sts.

   Note: When working past the antennae, make sure to push the antennae forward and work behind them instead of in front of them.

Rnd 11: (Sc 5, inc in next st) 6 times—42 sts.

Rnds 12–18: Sc in all 42 sts—42 sts.

Rnd 19: (Sc 5, dec) 6 times—36 sts.

Rnd 20: Sc 2, dec, (sc 4, dec) 5 times, sc 2—30 sts.

Rnd 21: (Sc 3, dec) 6 times—24 sts. Begin stuffing.

Rnd 22: Sc 1, dec, (sc 2, dec) 5 times, sc 1—18 sts.

Rnd 23: (Sc 1, dec) 6 times—12 sts.

Rnd 24: Dec in all sts—6 sts.

Fasten off with a slip stitch and use yarn needle to weave tail through the front loops of the remaining 6 stitches, pulling tightly to close the hole. Weave in tail.

Tail

In Color A:

Rnd 1: Start 7 sc in an adjustable ring—7 sts.

Rnds 2–5: Sc in all 7 sts—7 sts.

Rnd 6: Sc 2, dec, sc in next 3 sts—6 sts.

Rnd 7: Sc in all 6 sts—6 sts.

Fasten off with a slip stitch and leave a tail for sewing. Stuff lightly.

Feet (Make 4)

In Color A:

Rnd 1: Start 6 sc in an adjustable ring—6 sts.

Rnds 2–3: Sc in all 6 sts.

Fasten off with a slip stitch and leave a tail for sewing. Do not stuff.

Spots (Make 2)

In Color B:

Rnd 1: Start 6 sc in an adjustable ring—6 sts.

Rnd 2: Inc in all 6 sts—12 sts.

Fasten off with a slip stitch and leave a tail for sewing. Do not stuff.

Assembly

Pin and sew legs and tail to body as shown. Then sew spots onto back, as shown in main photo.

tank

Tank might look like he's a fairly sedentary cat, but you'd be wrong. He's actually one of the most active and athletic cats in the house; he's never met a sport he hasn't liked! Tank is always on the move, running somewhere—just be careful to stay out of his way while he's charging around. He's unstoppable!

FINISHED SIZE: 3in/7.5cm tall
(May vary depending on your hook size,
yarn type, and tension)

SKILL LEVEL: Intermediate

MATERIALS

- Lion Brand® Vanna's Choice® 3.5oz/100g,
  170yds/156m (100% acrylic)—one skein each:
  #860-149 Silver Gray (Color A), #860-153
  Black (Color B)
- Size D-3 (3.25mm) crochet hook
- Yarn needle
- 6mm safety eyes (2)
- Black embroidery floss (for nose and mouth)
- Polyester stuffing
- Wooden stuffing stick
- Stitch markers and pins

Head and Body

In Color A:

Rnd 1: Ch 11. Starting in second ch from hook,
sc in next 9 sts. Sc 4 into next st. On other side
of foundation ch, sc in next 8 sts. Sc 4 into next
st—25 sts.

Rnd 2: Sc 10, sc 3 into next st, inc in next st, sc in
next 11 sts, inc in next st, sc 3 into next s—31 sts.

Rnd 3: Sc 1, dec 4 times, sc 2, inc in next 3 sts, sc
in next 12 sts, inc in next 3 sts, sc 2—33 sts.

Rnd 4: Sc 3 into first st, (sc 1, sc 3 into next st) 3
times, sc in remaining 26 sts—41 sts.

Rnd 5: Sc in all 41 sts—41 sts.

Rnd 6: Sc 2, (inc in next st, sc 1) 6 times, sc in
remaining 27 sts—47 sts.

Rnds 7–10: Sc in all 47 sts—47 sts. Pause here to
place eyes and embroider nose and mouth. Eye
placement: between Rnds 3–4, approximately 3
sts apart.

Rnd 11: Inc in first st, (sc 4, inc in next st) 4 times, sc
3, inc in next st, sc in remaining 22 sts—53 sts.

Rnds 12–13: Sc in first 4 sts, change to Color B in
next st, sc in next 19 sts, change to Color A in next
st, sc in remaining 28 sts—53 sts.

Rnds 14–15: Sc in all 53 sts—53 sts.

Rnds 16–17: Sc in first 4 sts, change to Color B in
next st, sc in next 20 sts, change to Color A in next
st, sc in remaining 27 sts—53 sts.

Rnds 18–19: Sc in all 53 sts—53 sts.

Rnds 20–21: Sc in first 4 sts, change to Color B in
next st, sc in next 21 sts, change to Color A in next
st, sc in remaining 26 sts—53 sts.

Rnd 22: Sc in all 53 sts—53 sts.

Rnd 23: Sc 9, dec, (sc 8, dec) 4 times, sc 2—48 sts.

Rnd 24: Sc 3, dec, (sc 6, dec) 5 times, sc 3—42 sts.

Rnd 25: (Sc 5, dec) 6 times—36 sts.

Rnd 26: Sc 2, dec, (sc 4, dec) 5 times, sc 2—30 sts.
Begin stuffing.

Rnd 27: (Sc 3, dec) 6 times—24 sts.

Rnd 28: Sc 1, dec, (sc 2, dec) 5 times, sc 1—18 sts.

Rnd 29: (Sc 1, dec) 6 times—12 sts.

Rnd 30: Dec in all sts—6 sts.

Fasten off with a slip stitch and use yarn needle to weave tail through the front loops of the remaining 6 stitches, pulling tightly to close the hole. Weave in tail.

Feet (Make 4)

In Color A:

Rnd 1: Start 7 sc in an adjustable ring—7 sts.

Rnds 2–4: Sc in all 7 sts—7 sts.

Do not fasten off or stuff; press flat and single crochet through both sides to close. Yarn over and pull through to fasten off, leaving a tail for sewing.

Ears (Make 2)

In Color A:

Rnd 1: Start 5 sc in an adjustable ring—5 sts.

Rnd 2: Sc 1, inc in next st, sc 2, inc in next st—7 sts.

Rnd 3: Sc in all 7 sts—7 sts.

Rnd 4: Sc 2, inc in next st, sc 3, inc in next st—9 sts.

Fasten off with a slip stitch and leave a tail for sewing. Do not stuff; press flat.

Tail

In Color B:

Rnd 1: Start 8 sc in an adjustable ring—8 sts.

Rnds 2–4: Sc in all 8 sts—8 sts.

Rnd 5: Change to Color A in first st, sc in remaining 7 sts—8 sts.

Rnd 6: Sc in all 8 sts—8 sts.

Rnd 7: Sc 2, dec, sc in remaining 5 sts—7 sts.

Fasten off with a slip stitch and leave a tail for sewing. Stuff lightly.

ASSEMBLY

Pin and sew feet to body as shown.

Note: To keep Tank's feet from flopping around, after attaching the feet, thread your yarn through the foot and into the body below, as shown, a few times until secure.

Attach ears to body along Rnd 7, approximately 5 stitches apart.

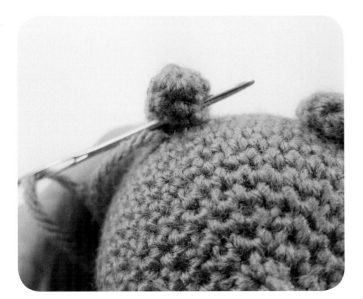

pudge

Pudge admires everything about fish, especially how calming and relaxing they are to watch. Normally Pudge is quite the anxious cat, but when he's dressed in his costume and parked in front of a fish bowl, he achieves a state of zen. Weird? Maybe a little, but it works.

FINISHED SIZE: 4in/10cm tall
(May vary depending on your hook size, yarn type, and tension)

SKILL LEVEL: Intermediate

MATERIALS

- Lion Brand® Vanna's Choice® 3.5oz/100g, 170yds/156m (100% acrylic)—one skein each: #860-099 Linen (Color A), #860-134 Terracotta (Color B), #860-153 Black (Color C), #860-100 White (Color D)
- Size D-3 (3.25mm) crochet hook
- Yarn needle
- 6mm safety eyes (2)
- Pink embroidery floss (for nose and mouth)
- Polyester stuffing
- Wooden stuffing stick
- Stitch markers and pins

Rnd 8: In **FLO** HDC in all 41 sts—41 sts.

Rnd 9: HDC in each st—41 sts.

Rnd 10: Insert hook into first st of round and into the corresponding leftover back loop from Rnd 8.

Head and Body

In Color A:

Rnd 1: Ch 7. Starting in second ch from hook, sc in next 5 sts. Sc 4 into next st. On other side of foundation ch, sc in next 4 sts, sc 4 into next st—17 sts.

Rnd 2: Sc 6, sc 3 into next st, inc in next st, sc 7, inc in next st, sc 3 into next st—23 sts.

Rnd 3: Sc 1, dec 2 times, sc 2, inc in next 3 sts, sc 8, inc in next 3 sts, sc 2—27 sts.

Rnd 4: Sc 3 into first 4 sts, sc in next 2 sts, (inc in next st, sc 1) 3 times, sc 8, (inc in next st, sc 1) 3 times, sc 1—41 sts.

Rnd 5: Sc in all 41 sts—41 sts.

Rnd 6: Sc 40. In last st, change to Color B—41 sts.

Rnd 7: Sc in all 41 sts—41 sts.

Complete a sc. Repeat in remaining 40 sts—41 sts.

Rnd 11: Sc in all 41 sts—41 sts. Pause here to place eyes and embroider nose and mouth. Eye placement: between Rnds 2–3, approximately 9 sts apart. Refer to photo on next page for eye placement.

Rnd 12: (Sc 4, inc in next st) 8 times, sc 1—49 sts.

Rnds 13–21: Sc in all 49 sts—49 sts.

Rnd 22: Sc 3, dec, (sc 6, dec) 5 times, sc 4—43 sts.

Rnd 23: (Sc 5, dec) 6 times, sc 1—37 sts.

Rnd 24: Sc 2, dec, (sc 4, dec) 5 times, sc 3—31 sts.

Rnd 25: (Sc 3, dec) 6 times, sc 1—25 sts. Begin stuffing.

Rnd 26: Sc 1, dec, (sc 2, dec) 5 times, sc 2—19 sts.

Rnd 27: (Sc 1, dec) 6 times, sc 1—13 sts.

Rnd 28: Dec 6 times, sc 1—7 sts.

Fasten off with a slip stitch and use yarn needle to weave tail through the front loops of the remaining 7 stitches, pulling tightly to close the hole. Weave in tail.

Top Fin

In Color B:

Rnd 1: Start 6 sc in an adjustable ring—6 sts.

Rnd 2: Inc in first 3 sts, sc 3—9 sts.

Rnd 3: Sc in all 9 sts—9 sts.

Rnd 4: (Sc 1, inc in next st) 3 times, sc 3—12 sts.

Rnd 5: Sc in all 12 sts—12 sts.

Do not fasten off or stuff; press flat and close top with 6 single crochet stitches. Yarn over and pull through to fasten off, leaving a tail for sewing.

Tail Fin (Make 2 pieces, then join)

In Color B:

Rnd 1: Start 6 sc in an adjustable ring—6 sts.

Rnd 2: (Sc 2, inc in next st) 2 times—8 sts.

Rnd 3: Sc in all 8 sts—8 sts.

Rnd 4: (Sc 3, inc in next st) 2 times—10 sts.

Rnd 5: Sc in all 10 sts—10 sts.

Rnd 6: (Sc 4, inc in next st) 2 times—12 sts.

When you finish the first fin, fasten off with a slip stitch and cut your yarn. When you finish the second, do not fasten off or cut your yarn.

With your loop still on your hook, insert your hook into the first stitch of the first fin.

Yarn over and complete a single crochet to join the two fins. Place your marker in this stitch and continue.

Rnd 7: Sc in remaining 23 sts—24 sts.

Rnd 8: (Sc 2, dec) 6 times—18 sts.

Rnd 9: Sc in first 5 sts. Press fins flat and sc through both sides across top to close.

Yarn over and pull through to fasten off, leaving a tail for sewing.

Fish Eyes (Make 2)

In Color C:

Rnd 1: Start 6 sc in an adjustable ring—6 sts.

Rnd 2: Inc in all 6 sts—12 sts.

Rnd 3: Change to Color D in first st. Inc in next st, (sc 1, inc in next st) 5 times—18 sts.

Rnds 4–5: Sc in all 18 sts—18 sts.

Fasten off with a slip stitch, leaving a tail for sewing. Stuff lightly.

Legs (Make 4)

In Color A:

Rnd 1: Start 8 sc in an adjustable ring—8 sts.

Rnds 2–4: Sc in all 8 sts—8 sts.

Fasten off with a slip stitch, leaving a tail for sewing. Stuff lightly.

Ears (Make 2)

In Color A:

Rnd 1: Start 5 sc in an adjustable ring—5 sts.

Rnd 2: Sc 1, inc in next st, sc 2, inc in next st—7 sts.

Rnd 3: Sc in all 7 sts—7 sts.

Rnd 4: Sc 2, inc in next st, sc 3, inc in next st—9 sts.

Do not fasten off or stuff; press flat and single crochet across top to close. Yarn over and pull through to fasten off, leaving a tail for sewing.

ASSEMBLY

Pin and sew pieces to body as shown.

Attach ears along Rnd 7.

chloe

Chloe sometimes finds it a bit hard to talk to the other cats; it's tricky when you're so much taller than everyone else! She's happy to reach high-up objects for them, though, and generously dispenses fashion advice to anyone who asks.

FINISHED SIZE: 5in/12.5cm tall
(May vary depending on your hook size,
yarn type, and tension)

SKILL LEVEL: Intermediate

MATERIALS

- Lion Brand® Vanna's Choice® 3.5oz/100g,
  170yds/156m (100% acrylic)—one skein each:
  #860-405 Silver Heather (Color A), #860-147
  Purple (Color B), #860-146 Dusty Purple
  (Color C)
- Size D-3 (3.25mm) crochet hook
- Yarn needle
- 6mm safety eyes (2)
- Pink embroidery floss (for nose and mouth)
- Polyester stuffing
- Wooden stuffing stick
- Stitch markers and pins

Head and Body

Starting in Color A:

Rnd 1: Ch 5. Starting in second ch from hook, sc 3.
Sc 4 into next st. On other side of foundation chain,
sc 2. Sc 4 into next st—13 sts.

Rnd 2: Sc 4, sc 3 into next st, inc in next st, sc 5, inc
in next st, sc 3 into next st—19 sts.

Rnd 3: Sc 5, inc in next 3 st, sc 7, inc in next 3 st, sc
1—25 sts.

Rnd 4: Sc 6, (inc in next st, sc 1) 3 times, sc 7, (inc in
next st, sc 1) 3 times—31 sts.

Rnd 5: Sc 7, (inc in next st, sc 2) 3 times, sc 6, (inc
in next st, sc 2) 3 times—37 sts.

Rnds 6–8: Sc in all 37 sts—37 sts.

Rnd 9: Sc 8, (inc in next st, sc 3) 3 times, sc 6, (inc
in next st, sc 3) 2 times, inc in next st, sc 2—43 sts.

Rnds 10–11: Sc in all 43 sts—43 sts.

Rnd 12: Sc 8, (dec, sc in next 3 sts) 3 times, sc 6,
(dec, sc 3) 2 times, dec, sc 2—37 sts.

Rnd 13: Sc in all 37 sts—37 sts.

Rnd 14: Sc 7, (dec, sc 2) 3 times, sc 6, (dec, sc 2)
3 times—31 sts.

Rnd 15: Sc 6, (dec, sc 1) 3 times, sc 7, (dec, sc 1)
3 times—25 sts. Pause here to place eyes and
embroider nose and mouth. Eye placement:
between Rnds 10–11 and 5 sts apart.

Rnd 16: Sc 1, dec, (sc 2, dec) 5 times, sc 2—19 sts.
Begin stuffing.

Rnd 17: (Sc 1, dec) 6 times, sc 1—13 sts.

Rnd 18: In **BLO** change to Color B in first st, sc
in remaining 12 sts—13 sts. The remaining front
loops from this round will be used to make the
turtleneck of the sweater after you have completed
the body.

Rnd 19: Sc 5, inc in next st, sc 6, inc in next st—15
sts.

Rnd 20: Sc in all 15 sts—15 sts.

Rnd 21: (Sc 4, inc in next st) 3 times—18 sts.

Rnd 22: Change to Color C in first st, sc in remaining 17 sts—18 sts.

Rnd 23: (Sc 5, inc in next st) 3 times—21 sts.

Rnds 24–25: Sc in all 21 sts—21 sts.

Rnd 26: Change to Color B in first st. Sc in next 5 sts, inc in next st. (Sc 6, inc in next st) 2 times—24 sts.

Rnds 27–29: Sc in all 24 sts—24 sts.

Rnd 30: Change to Color C in first st. Sc in next 6 sts, inc in next st. (Sc 7, inc in next st) 2 times—27 sts.

Rnds 31–32: Sc in all 27 sts—27 sts.

Rnd 33: In **FLO** sc in all 27 sts—27 sts.

Rnd 34: In remaining back loops of Rnd 33: In first st, change to Color A. Sc in remaining 26 sts—27 sts. Begin stuffing.

Rnd 35: (Sc 7, dec) 3 times—24 sts.

Rnd 36: Sc 1, dec, (sc 2, dec) 5 times, sc 1—18 sts.

Rnd 37: (Sc 1, dec) 6 times—12 sts.

Rnd 38: Dec in all sts—6 sts.

Fasten off with a slip stitch and use yarn needle to weave tail through the front loops of the remaining 6 stitches, pulling tightly to close the hole. Weave in tail.

Turtleneck

Make a slipknot of Color B on your hook. Insert hook into first leftover front loop of Rnd 18 and join yarn.

Continue:

Rnds 1–2: HDC in each st—13 sts.

Fasten off with a slip stitch and weave in ends.

Beret

In Color B:

Rnd 1: Start 6 sc in an adjustable ring—6 sts.

Rnd 2: Inc in all 6 sts—12 sts.

Rnd 3: (Sc 1, inc in next st) 6 times—18 sts.

Rnd 4: Sc 1, inc, (sc 2, inc in next st) 5 times, sc 1—24 sts.

Rnd 5: Sc in all 24 sts—24 sts.

Rnd 6: Dec in all 24 sts—12 sts.

Fasten off with a slip stitch, leaving a tail for sewing.

Beret Top

With Color B, make a slipknot and leave a tail of at least 3in/7.6cm. Chain 3. Starting in second chain from hook, slip stitch 2. Fasten off, leaving a tail. Thread your yarn tails onto a yarn needle and weave them through the top of the beret. Knot the two tails together tightly 2–3 times to secure. Stuff beret lightly.

Tail

In Color A:

Rnd 1: Start 7 sc in an adjustable ring—7 sts.

Rnds 2–7: Sc in all 7 sts—7 sts.

Rnd 8: Sc 2, dec, sc in remaining 3 sts—6 sts.

Rnd 9: Sc in all 6 sts—6 sts.

Fasten off with a slip stitch, leaving a tail for sewing. Stuff lightly.

Ear (Make 1)

In Color A:

Rnd 1: Start 5 sc in an adjustable ring—5 sts.

Rnd 2: Sc 1, inc in next st, sc 2, inc in next st—7 sts.

Rnd 3: Sc in all 7 sts—7 sts.

Rnd 4: Sc 2, inc in next st, sc 3, inc in next st—9 sts.

Rnd 5: Sc in all 9 sts—9 sts.

Fasten off with a slip stitch, leaving a tail for sewing. Do not stuff; press flat.

Back Legs (Make 2)

In Color A:

Rnd 1: Start 6 sc in an adjustable ring—6 sts.

Rnds 2–3: Sc in all 6 sts—6 sts.

Do not fasten off or stuff; press flat and close top with 2 single crochet stitches. Yarn over and pull through to fasten off, leaving a tail for sewing.

Front Legs (Make 2)

In Color A:

Rnd 1: Start 6 sc in an adjustable ring—6 sts.

Rnds 2–3: Sc in all 6 sts—6 sts.

Rnd 4: Change to Color C in first st, sc in remaining 5 sts—6 sts.

Rnds 5–10: Sc in all 6 sts—6 sts.

Do not fasten off or stuff; press flat and close top with 2 single crochet stitches. Yarn over and pull through to fasten off, leaving a tail for sewing.

ASSEMBLY

Pin and sew pieces to body as shown.

bug

Watch out for Bug—she might be the smallest cat in the house, but she is not to be reckoned with! Bug is quite bossy and manages to convince the other cats to do things for her; she gets away with it because she's so cute.

FINISHED SIZE: 1½in/4cm tall
(May vary depending on your hook size,
yarn type, and tension)

SKILL LEVEL: Easy

MATERIALS

- Lion Brand® Vanna's Choice® 3.5oz/100g,
  170yds/156m (100% acrylic)—one skein each:
  #860-125 Taupe (Color A), #860-123 Beige
  (Color B)

- Size D-3 (3.25mm) crochet hook

- Yarn needle

- 6mm safety eyes (2)

- Dark brown embroidery floss
  (for nose and mouth)

- Polyester stuffing

- Wooden stuffing stick

- Stitch markers and pins

Rnds 6–9: Sc in all 24 sts—24 sts.

Rnd 10: Sc 1, dec, (sc 2, dec) 5 times, sc 1—18 sts.

Rnd 11: (Sc 1, dec) 6 times—12 sts. Begin stuffing.

Rnd 12: Dec in all sts—6 sts.

Fasten off with a slip stitch and use yarn needle to
weave tail through the front loops of the remaining
6 stitches, pulling tightly to close the hole. Weave
in tail.

Head and Body

Starting in Color A:

Rnd 1: Ch 4. Starting in second ch from hook, sc 2.
Sc 4 into next st. On other side of foundation chain,
sc 1, sc 4 into next st—11 sts.

Rnd 2: Change to Color B in first st. Sc in next 2 sts,
sc 3 into next st, inc in next st, sc 4, inc in next st, sc
3 into next st—17 sts.

Rnd 3: Inc in first 4 sts, sc in remaining 13 sts—21
sts.

Rnd 4: Sc in all 21 sts—21 sts.

Rnd 5: Sc 1, (inc in next st, sc 1) 3 times, sc in
remaining 14 sts—24 sts. Pause here to place
eyes and embroider nose and mouth. Eye
placement: between Rnds 1–2, approximately 3
sts apart.

Ears (Make 2)

In Color A:

Rnd 1: Start 5 sc in an adjustable ring—5 sts.

Rnd 2: Sc 1, inc in next st, sc 2, inc in next st—7 sts.

Rnd 3: Sc in all 7 sts—7 sts.

Do not fasten off or stuff; press flat and close top
with 3 single crochet stitches. Yarn over and pull
through to fasten off, leaving a tail for sewing.

Feet (Make 4)

In Color A:

Make a slip knot, leaving a long tail. Ch 2.

In second ch from hook, HDC 4.

Drop loop from hook, reinsert hook into first HDC, grab loop and draw through.

Yarn over and pull through to secure. Fasten off and leave a tail. Knot both tails together.

Tail

In Color A:

Rnd 1: Start 5 sc in an adjustable ring—5 sts.

Rnds 2–4: Sc in all 5 sts—5 sts.

Fasten off with a slip stitch, leaving a tail for sewing.

ASSEMBLY

Pin and sew pieces to body as shown. Attach ears between Rnds 4–5.

felipe

Next to Chloe, Felipe is the second most fashion-forward cat in the house. He dresses up as anything, as long as his best friend Tia can wear something similar to match. Today he has decided to be a very chic prince!

FINISHED SIZE: 4in/10cm tall
(May vary depending on your hook size, yarn type, and tension)

SKILL LEVEL: Intermediate

MATERIALS

- Lion Brand® Vanna's Choice® 3.5oz/100g, 170yds/156m (100% acrylic)—one skein each: #860-100 White (Color A), 860-106 Aquamarine (Color B), #860-176 Peacock (Color C), #860-171 Fern (Color D), #860-158 Mustard (Color E)
- Size D-3 (3.25mm) crochet hook
- Yarn needle
- 6mm safety eyes (2)
- Pink embroidery floss (for nose and mouth)
- Polyester stuffing
- Wooden stuffing stick
- Stitch markers and pins

Head and Body

In Color A:

Rnd 1: Ch 5. Starting in second ch from hook, sc 3. Sc 4 into next st. On other side of foundation chain, sc 2. Sc 4 into next st—13 sts.

Rnd 2: Sc 4, sc 3 into next st, inc in next st, sc 5, inc in next st, sc 3 into next st—19 sts.

Rnd 3: Sc 5, inc in next 3 st, sc 7, inc in next 3 st, sc 1—25 sts.

Rnd 4: (Sc 4, inc in next st) 5 times—30 sts.

Rnds 5–6: Sc in all 30 sts—30 sts.

Rnd 7: (Sc 5, inc in next st) 5 times—35 sts.

Rnds 8–11: Sc in all 35 sts—35 sts.

Rnd 12: (Sc 5, dec) 5 times—30 sts.

Rnd 13: (Sc 3, dec) 6 times—24 sts. Pause here to place eyes and embroider nose and mouth. Eye placement: between Rnds 7–8, 4 sts apart.

Rnd 14: Sc 1, dec, (sc 2, dec) 5 times, sc 1—18 sts. Begin stuffing.

Rnd 15: (Sc 1, dec) 6 times—12 sts.

Rnd 16: In **BLO** sc in all 12 sts—12 sts.

Rnd 17: In **FLO** change to Color B in first st, sc 2, inc in next st, (sc 3, inc in next st) 2 times—15 sts.

Rnd 18: (Sc 4, inc in next st) 3 times—18 sts.

Rnds 19–20: Sc in all 18 sts—18 sts.

Rnd 21: In first st, change to Color C. Sc in next st, inc in next st. (Sc 2, inc in next st) 5 times—24 sts.

Rnd 22: In **FLO** sc in all 24 sts—24 sts.

Rnd 23: In leftover back loops of Rnd 22, sc in all 24 sts—24 sts.

Rnds 24–25: Sc in all 24 sts—24 sts.

Rnd 26: (Sc 2, dec) 6 times—18 sts. Begin stuffing.

Rnd 27: (Sc 1, dec) 6 times—12 sts.

Rnd 28: Dec in all sts—6 sts.

Fasten off with a slip stitch and use yarn needle to weave tail through the front loops of the remaining 6 stitches, pulling tightly to close the hole. Weave in tail.

Cape

Make a slipknot of Color D on your hook, leaving a tail long enough to weave in later. Insert hook into first leftover front loop of Rnd 16, join yarn and continue, referring to photos on next page.

Rnd 1: (Sc 1, inc in next st) 6 times—18 sts.

> **Note:** You will now be working in rows.

Row 2: Sc 8, ch 1 and turn—8 sts.

Row 3: Sc 7 until you reach marker. Remove marker and sc in next 3 sts. Ch 1 and turn—10 sts.

Row 6: Sc in all 13 sts.

Fasten off and weave in ends.

Back Legs (Make 2)

In Color A:

Rnd 1: Start 5 sc in an adjustable ring—5 sts.

Rnd 2: Sc in all 5 sts—5 sts.

Rnd 3: Sc 4, change to Color C in last st—5 sts.

Rnd 4: Inc in all 5 sts—10 sts.

Fasten off with a slip stitch, leaving a tail for sewing. Stuff lightly.

Front Legs (Make 2)

In Color A:

Rnd 1: Start 5 sc in an adjustable ring—5 sts.

Rnd 2: Sc in all 5 sts—5 sts.

Rnd 3: Sc 4, change to Color B in last st—5 sts.

Rnd 4: Sc 1, inc in next st, sc 2, inc in next st—7 sts.

Rnds 5–7: Sc in all 7 sts—7 sts.

Do not fasten off or stuff; press flat and close top with 2 single crochet stitches. Yarn over and pull through to fasten off, leaving a tail for sewing.

Ears (Make 2)

In Color A:

Rnd 1: Start 5 sc in an adjustable ring—5 sts.

Rnd 2: Sc 1, inc in next st, sc 2, inc in next st—7 sts.

Rnd 3: Sc in all 7 sts—7 sts.

Rnd 4: Sc 2, inc in next st, sc 3, inc in next st—9 sts.

Rnd 5: Sc in all 9 sts—9 sts.

Fasten off with a slip stitch, leaving a tail for sewing. Do not stuff; press flat.

Tail

In Color A:

Rnd 1: Start 6 sc in an adjustable ring—6 sts.

Rnds 2–5: Sc in all 6 sts—6 sts.

Fasten off with a slip stitch, leaving a tail for sewing. Do not stuff.

Row 4: Sc 10. Ch 1 and turn—10 sts.

Row 5: Inc in first st, sc 3, inc in next st, sc 4, inc in next st. Ch 1 and turn—13 sts.

Crown

In Color E:

Rnd 1: Ch 14. Join first and last ch with a slip stitch, making sure not to twist the chain—14 sts.

Rnd 2: Sc in all 14 sts—14 sts.

Rnd 3: (Sc in next st, ch 2, slst in next st) 7 times.

Fasten off with a slip stitch, leaving a tail for sewing.

ASSEMBLY

Sew back legs and tail to body as shown.

Sew front legs to body in the round directly under the cape, with a space of one stitch between them.

Sew ears to the top of the head with about 5 stitches between them, then place crown over one of the ears and sew it to the head to secure it.

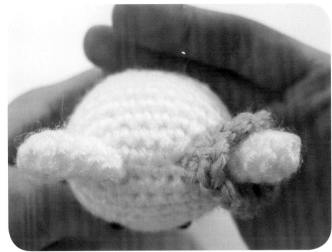

tia

Tia actually doesn't care for playing dress-up, but she loves spending time with her best friend Felipe, so she does it anyway. What a good friend! Tia actually would rather be a doctor, if she had to choose—but for today, she'll be a princess.

FINISHED SIZE: 4in/10cm tall
(May vary depending on your hook size, yarn type, and tension)

SKILL LEVEL: Intermediate

MATERIALS

- Lion Brand® Vanna's Choice® 3.5oz/100g, 170yds/156m (100% acrylic)—one skein each: #860-098 Fisherman (Color A), #860-191 Lilac (Color B), #860-183 Periwinkle (Color C), #860-112 Raspberry (Color D), #860-405 Silver Heather (Color E)
- Size D-3 (3.25mm) crochet hook
- Yarn needle
- 6mm safety eyes (2)
- Pink embroidery floss (for nose and mouth)
- Black embroidery floss (for eyelashes)
- Polyester stuffing
- Wooden stuffing stick
- Stitch markers and pins

Head and Body

In Color A:

Rnd 1: Ch 5. Starting in second ch from hook, sc 3. Sc 4 into next st. On other side of foundation chain, sc 2. Sc 4 into next st—13 sts.

Rnd 2: Sc 4, sc 3 into next st, inc in next st, sc 5, inc in next st, sc 3 into next st—19 sts.

Rnd 3: Sc 5, inc in next 3 st, sc 7, inc in next 3 st, sc 1—25 sts.

Rnd 4: (Sc 4, inc in next st) 5 times—30 sts.

Rnds 5–6: Sc in all 30 sts—30 sts.

Rnd 7: (Sc 5, inc in next st) 5 times—35 sts.

Rnds 8–11: Sc in all 35 sts—35 sts.

Rnd 12: (Sc 5, dec) 5 times—30 sts.

Rnd 13: (Sc 3, dec) 6 times—24 sts. Pause here to place eyes and embroider nose, mouth, and eyelashes as in main photo. Eye placement: between Rnds 7–8, 6 sts apart.

Rnd 14: Sc 1, dec, (sc 2, dec) 5 times, sc 1—18 sts. Begin stuffing head.

Rnd 15: (Sc 1, dec) 6 times—12 sts.

Rnd 16: Sc in all 12 sts—12 sts.

Rnd 17: In **FLO** change to Color B in first st, sc in remaining 11 sts—12 sts.

Rnd 18: (Sc 3, inc in next st) 3 times—15 sts.

Rnd 19: (Sc 4, inc in next st) 3 times—18 sts.

Rnd 20: Sc in all 18 sts—18 sts.

Rnd 21: In **BLO** sc in all 18 sts—18 sts. The remaining front loops will be used to attach the belt to the dress once it is complete.

Rnd 22: In **FLO** change to Color C in first st. Inc in next st, (sc 2, inc in next st) 5 times, sc 1—24 sts. When you finish the round, drop your loop from your hook and place a stitch marker in it to save your spot. You'll continue the dress later, but first, you'll complete the body underneath. Continue.

99

Rnd 23: In remaining back loops of Rnd 22: In first st, join Color A.

Place marker in this stitch. Inc in next st. (Sc 2, inc) 5 times, sc 1—24 sts.

Rnds 24–25: Sc in all 24 sts—24 sts.

Rnd 26: Sc 1, dec, (sc 2, dec) 5 times, sc 1—18 sts.

Rnd 27: (Sc 1, dec) 6 times—12 sts. Stuff the body.

Rnd 28: Dec in all sts—6 sts.

Fasten off with a slip stitch and use yarn needle to weave tail through the front loops of the remaining 6 stitches, pulling tightly to close the hole. Weave in tail.

Pick up the loop of Color C that you dropped at the end of Rnd 22 and continue the dress:

Rnd 29: (Sc 3, inc in next st) 6 times—30 sts.

Rnd 30: Sc in all 30 sts—30 sts.

Rnd 31: Sc 2, inc in next st, (sc 4, inc in next st) 5 times, sc 2—36 sts.

Rnds 32–33: Sc in all 36 sts—36 sts.

Rnd 34: (HDC 3 into next st, slst into next st) 18 times to create dress edging.

Fasten off with a slip stitch and weave in ends.

Dress Belt

Make a slipknot of Color D on your hook, leaving a tail long enough to weave in later. Insert hook into first leftover front loop of Rnd 21, join yarn and continue:

Rnd 1: (Sc 2, inc in next st) 6 times—24 sts.

Fasten off with a slip stitch and weave in ends.

Back Legs (Make 2):

In Color A:

Rnd 1: Start 5 sc in an adjustable ring—5 sts.

Rnds 2–3: Sc in all 5 sts—5 sts.

Fasten off with a slip stitch, leaving a tail for sewing. Do not stuff.

Front Legs (Make 2)

In Color A:

Rnd 1: Start 5 sc in an adjustable ring—5 sts.

Rnd 2: Sc in all 5 sts—5 sts.

Rnd 3: Sc 4, change to Color B in next st—5 sts.

Rnd 4: Sc 1, inc in next st, sc in remaining 3 sts —6 sts.

Rnd 5: Sc in all 6 sts—6 sts.

Do not fasten off or stuff; press flat and close top with 2 single crochet stitches. Yarn over and pull through to fasten off, leaving a tail for sewing.

Ears (Make 2)

In Color A:

Rnd 1: Start 5 sc in an adjustable ring—5 sts.

Rnd 2: Sc 1, inc in next st, sc 2, inc in next st—7 sts.

Rnd 3: Sc in all 7 sts—7 sts.

Rnd 4: Sc 2, inc in next st, sc 3, inc in next st—9 sts.

Rnd 5: Sc in all 9 sts—9 sts.

Fasten off with a slip stitch, leaving a tail for sewing. Do not stuff; press flat.

Tail

In Color A:

Rnd 1: Start 6 sc in an adjustable ring—6 sts.

Rnds 2–5: Sc in all 6 sts—6 sts.

Fasten off with a slip stitch, leaving a tail for sewing. Do not stuff.

Crown

In Color E:

Rnd 1: Ch 8. Join first and last ch with a slip stitch, making sure not to twist the chain—8 sts.

Rnd 2: Sc in all 8 sts—8 sts.

Rnd 3: (Sc in next st, ch 2, slst in next st) 4 times.

Fasten off with a slip stitch, leaving a tail for sewing.

ASSEMBLY

Pin and then sew back legs to body as shown.

Sew ears to top of head with approximately 5 stitches in between. Sew crown to head directly between ears as shown in main photo on page 98.

poe

Poe is like a shadow, or a little ghost—he's very shy, so you may only see him out of the corner of your eye for a second before he disappears again. The other cats aren't even sure he exists!

FINISHED SIZE: 2¾in/7cm tall
(May vary depending on your hook size, yarn type, and tension)

SKILL LEVEL: Easy

MATERIALS

- Lion Brand® Vanna's Choice® 3.5oz/100g, 170yds/156m (100% acrylic)—one skein #860-153 Black (Color A)
- Size D-3 (3.25mm) crochet hook
- Yarn needle
- 6mm safety eyes (2)
- Pink embroidery floss (for nose and mouth)
- Black embroidery floss (for eyelashes)
- Polyester stuffing
- Wooden stuffing stick
- Stitch markers and pins

Head and Body

In Color A:

Rnd 1: Ch 4. Starting in second ch from hook, sc 2. Sc 4 into next st. On other side of foundation chain, sc 1, sc 4 into next st—11 sts.

Rnd 2: Sc 3, sc 3 into next st, inc in next st, sc 4, inc in next st, sc 3 into next st—17 sts.

Rnd 3: (Sc 3, inc in next st) 4 times, sc 1—21 sts.

Rnd 4: (Sc 6, inc in next st) 3 times—24 sts.

Rnds 5–6: Sc in all 24 sts—24 sts.

Rnd 7: (Sc 5, inc in next st) 4 times—28 sts.

Rnd 8: Sc in each st—28 sts.

Rnd 9: (Sc 2, dec) 7 times—21 sts. Pause here to place eyes and embroider nose and mouth. Eye placement: between Rnds 7–8, 3 sts apart.

Make a Cardboard Box for your Dumpling Cat— see Bonus Pattern on page 105

Rnd 10: (Sc 5, dec) 3 times—18 sts.

Rnd 11: (Sc 1, dec) 6 times—12 sts. Begin stuffing the head.

Rnd 12: (Sc 2, dec) 3 times—9 sts.

Rnd 13: (Sc 2, inc in next st) 3 times—12 sts.

Rnd 14: Sc in all 12 sts—12 sts.

Rnd 15: (Sc 3, inc in next st) 3 times—15 sts.

Rnds 16–17: Sc in all 15 sts—15 sts.

Rnd 18: (Sc 1, dec) 5 times—10 sts. Stuff the body.

Rnd 19: Dec in all sts—5 sts.

Fasten off with a slip stitch and use yarn needle to weave tail through the front loops of the remaining 5 stitches, pulling tightly to close the hole. Weave in tail.

Front Legs (Make 2)

In Color A:

Rnd 1: Start 5 sc in an adjustable ring—5 sts.

Rnds 2–3: Sc in all 5 sts—5 sts.

Do not fasten off; press flat and close top with 2 single crochet stitches. Yarn over and pull through to fasten off, leaving a tail for sewing.

Back Legs (Make 2)

In Color A:

Rnd 1: Start 5 sc in an adjustable ring—5 sts.

Rnd 2: Sc in all 5 sts—5 sts.

Do not fasten off or stuff; press flat and close top with 2 single crochet stitches. Yarn over and pull through to fasten off, leaving a tail for sewing.

Ears (Make 2)

In Color A:

Rnd 1: Start 5 sc in an adjustable ring—5 sts.

Rnd 2: Sc 1, inc in next st, sc 2, inc in next st—7 sts.

Rnd 3: Sc in all 7 sts—7 sts.

Do not fasten off; press flat and close top with 2–3 single crochet stitches. Yarn over and pull through to fasten off, leaving a tail for sewing.

Tail

In Color A:

Rnd 1: Start 5 sc in an adjustable ring—5 sts.

Rnds 2–4: Sc in all 5 sts—5 sts.

Fasten off, leaving a tail for sewing. Do not stuff.

ASSEMBLY

Sew tail and back legs to bottom of body as shown in photos.

Sew front legs to body, right below the neck, with about one stitch between. Sew ears to top of head as shown.

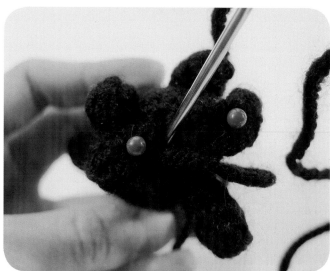

cardboard box

FINISHED SIZE: 2¼in/5.5cm by 3¾in/9.5cm (May vary depending on your hook size, yarn type, and tension)

SKILL LEVEL: Easy

MATERIALS

- Lion Brand® Vanna's Choice® 3.5oz/100g, 170yds/156m (100% acrylic)—one skein: #860-130 Honey (Color A)
- Size D-3 (3.25mm) crochet hook
- Yarn needle
- Stitch marker

Box Bottom

Row 1: Ch 17. Starting in second ch from hook, sc 16. Ch 1 and turn—16 sts.

Rows 2–18: Sc in each st across. Ch 1 and turn—16 sts.

Fasten off. Turn piece clockwise and insert hook into stitch as shown.

Join new piece of yarn and single crochet 1 in this stitch, insert marker and continue.

Single crochet across edge of box for 16 stitches.

105

Single crochet 3 into next (17th) stitch.
Single crochet in next 14 stitches.

In next stitch (15th stitch), single crochet 3. Single crochet in next 15 stitches.

Single crochet 3 in next stitch (16th stitch). Single crochet in next 14 stitches. In 15th stitch, single crochet 3—71 sts.

You've now reached the marker. Proceed to work in rounds, beginning in the stitch with the marker:

Rnd 1: In **BLO** sc in each st—71 sts.

Rnds 2–14: Sc in each st—71 sts.

Box Flaps (Make 4)

Row 1: Ch 17. Starting in second ch from hook, sc 16. Ch 1 and turn.

Rows 2–9: Sc in each st across. Ch 1 and turn—16 sts.

Do not fasten off. Single crochet around the perimeter of the flap, along the edges, until you have worked around the entire piece once. Fasten off and leave a tail for sewing.

ASSEMBLY

Use leftover tails to whipstitch flaps to top of cardboard box.